Mary McMurtrie's
Country Garden Flowers

Mary McMurtrie's
Country Garden Flowers

Timothy Clark

GARDEN • ART • PRESS

ISBN 978-1-87067-360-0

British Library Cataloguing-in-Publication Data
A catalogue record for this book is available from the British Library

Frontispiece. 1. *Ranunculus aconitifolius* Fair Maids of France (Kent). 2. *Aquilegia* Granny's Bonnet, double. 3. *Bellis perennis* 'Alice', double daisy. 4. *Bellis perennis* 'Prolifera' – Hen and Chickens daisy. 5. *Bellis perennis* 'Dresden China', double daisy, pink. 6. *Bellis perennis* 'Robert', double daisy, white.

Title page. Auricula 'Old Aberdeenshire Yellow'.

Printed and bound in Great Britain by Butler Tanner and Dennis, Frome, Somerset
for Garden Art Press, an imprint of Antique Collectors' Club Ltd., Woodbridge, Suffolk

CONTENTS

FOREWORD

'It is much the rage to obtain new plants and neglect old ones' was an observation in 1848 by George Glenny that might equally well have been attributed to Mary McMurtrie a hundred years later. The author of a *Handbook of Practical Gardening* (1851) he was, like Mary McMurtrie, greatly concerned that many of the well-known varieties of much loved garden plants of his era were being lost as gardeners replaced them with newer introductions.

Her passion for collecting, growing and making available for other gardeners old-fashioned flowers and cottage garden plants, an enthusiasm shared with her husband, the Reverend John McMurtrie, is admirably chronicled and encapsulated in this account of her life and achievements by Timothy Clark, a long-time correspondent and friend of Mary McMurtrie who shares the same zeal for saving and preserving historic garden plants.

Mary McMurtrie corresponded with many other renowned gardeners like Margery Fish, who were also collecting, propagating and exchanging their treasured double primroses, old pinks and auriculas as well as many other uncommon varieties of old cottage garden plants. These became more widely available to other interested gardeners through her nursery specialising in old garden flowers and alpines which she ran for over forty years. So well before the formation of the NCCPG (The National Council for the Conservation of Plants and Gardens), now to be called Plant Heritage, a much more appropriate name, Mary McMurtrie was bringing to the attention of the wider gardening public the need to grow, and thus save and conserve, these plants from the past which were, and still are, historically important and often aesthetically attractive garden plants.

She was also a very accomplished botanical artist, as may be seen from her delightful watercolour paintings of the flowers she grew in her several gardens and of wildflowers in the Scottish countryside, many of which are reproduced here as well as in her books on *Scots Roses* and *Old Cottage Pinks* which provide invaluable records of the historic variants of *Rosa spinosissima*, the Scots Rose and the old, fragrant pinks that she had found in various gardens in Scotland or received from her many correspondents and other gardening friends.

As a long-time proponent of the need to conserve our old garden plants I am particularly pleased to have been asked to contribute this Foreword to Timothy Clark's tribute to Mary McMurtrie which celebrates the life and achievements of one of the most versatile and remarkable gardeners and botanical artists of her generation.

Chris Brickell
Former Director of the RHS Garden, Wisley and
Director General of the Royal Horticultural Society

CHAPTER 1
The Life of Mary McMurtrie

Plate 1. Mary Margaret Mitchell, aged about six.

The daughter of the village schoolmaster in Skene, Aberdeenshire, she was born in 1902 and christened Mary Margaret Mitchell (well into her nineties she was still complaining there were too many Ms in her name). Deciding to pursue a career in painting, she enrolled at Gray's School of Art in Aberdeen where she greatly enjoyed the course which covered all aspects of art, including drawing from life. She graduated first in her year and succeeded in getting both the head of the art school and the head of the painting department to sit for her while she drew them; she then went on to make etchings of the portraits.

Despite her enthusiasm for painting, she went for a year to the School of Domestic Science (where she disliked the constraint after the freedom of the art school). This was at the insistence of her mother who felt it was essential training for married life in a manse, which Mary was about to experience, marrying John McMurtrie, the Church of Scotland minister at Skene, in 1924. After marriage she continued with her etching for a short period, but four

children to bring up and a busy parish to run meant that there was little time for etching and painting. Her overriding interest became gardening and this represented a strong link between her and her husband.

John McMurtrie remembered from his childhood the story of *Mary's Meadow* by Juliana Ewing, printed as a children's comic in *Aunt Judy's Magazine* from November 1883 to March 1884 and as a book in 1886. It tells a story of a sensible older child who attempts to keep her younger brothers and sister entertained with games. Inspired by John Parkinson's *Paradisi in Sole Paradisus Terrestris,* she invents characters for them to play in creating their own paradise within their parents' garden. They chose hardy cottage garden perennials and wildflowers. Mary's role in the game was Traveller's Joy, to put garden plants in places for people without gardens to enjoy, and hose-in-hose cowslips (named after the hose Elizabethan gentlemen wore, frequently seen in

Plate 2. Mary Margaret Mitchell, aged about ten.

Plate 3. Skene Manse, June 1914. Left to right John's mother, John McMurtrie, Mary's mother and Mary herself, aged twelve.

Tudor portraits) were planted in a meadow near her house. She was subsequently turned out of the meadow by the Squire, but they were brought together by the dog called Saxon. The story was so popular that it inspired the creation of the Parkinson Society for lovers of old hardy flowers. They circulated old gardening books to try to prevent the extermination of rare wild flowers and to keep in cultivation the plants of past centuries.

The influence of this book could be seen in the garden of the Manse at Skene where the McMurtries grew many native hardy plants, with John being especially fond of primroses. He exchanged plants with all the main growers of the day: Eda Hume, who had written on primroses for Sacheverell Sitwell's book of *Old Fashioned Flowers;* Captain Hawkes, whose seed of gold laced polyanthus was sent to Barnhaven to found the gold laced polyanthus we see in

garden centres today; Mrs. Emmerson and fellow amateur hybridists like William Chalmers of Blackbutts Nursery, Stonehaven, Kincardineshire. William Cocker of the Aberdeen rose firm, James Cocker Ltd, was a particular friend. He had used pollen of the deep violet semi-double primrose 'Arthur du Moulin' to raise almost fifty double hybrids. He only named twelve for commerce, but he gave the rest of them to friends. Sir Herbert Maxwell, in his *Scottish Gardens,* stated William Cocker was more concerned with natural species than florists' varieties. Cockers was the principal nursery in Scotland at the time and the Bon Accord primroses still linger today with the memories of primroses before they became too large. The reason this strain of primroses did not become more widespread nationally is that they did not take kindly to alkaline conditions in many parts of the

13ᵗʰ July 24

Plate 4. John McMurtrie, pencil drawing by Mary, 1924.

country, but John McMurtrie treasured them in his collection.

The nursery started at Skene Manse as a joint venture in 1931; before this time John McMurtrie had sold saxifrages and double primroses to growers in both England and Ireland. Designing the garden, weeding, planting and dividing were occupations Mary enjoyed in the long summer evenings. At the beginning of the war she commenced breeding Dark Cuckoo Maran chickens; the growing children loved the brown eggs. John grew his vegetables and had his primrose beds and, despite the war, they both persevered in preserving the older varieties of plants which were their mutual interest.

Mary had loved plants and gardens from childhood, inspired by her parents, but the real inspiration for her gardening came from her husband's love of plants. I remember that one of Margery Fish's relatives asked her, when she wrote *We Made A Garden,* why not call it the garden you made for Walter? Christopher Lloyd remarked to me that both Mary McMurtrie and Margery Fish really developed their talents for gardening, writing and painting only after their respective husbands had died. Gladys Emmerson, despite her comfortable living as a writer and illustrator before her marriage, had no desire to work other than to please her husband, the surgeon Lindsay Emmerson. Her joy was to

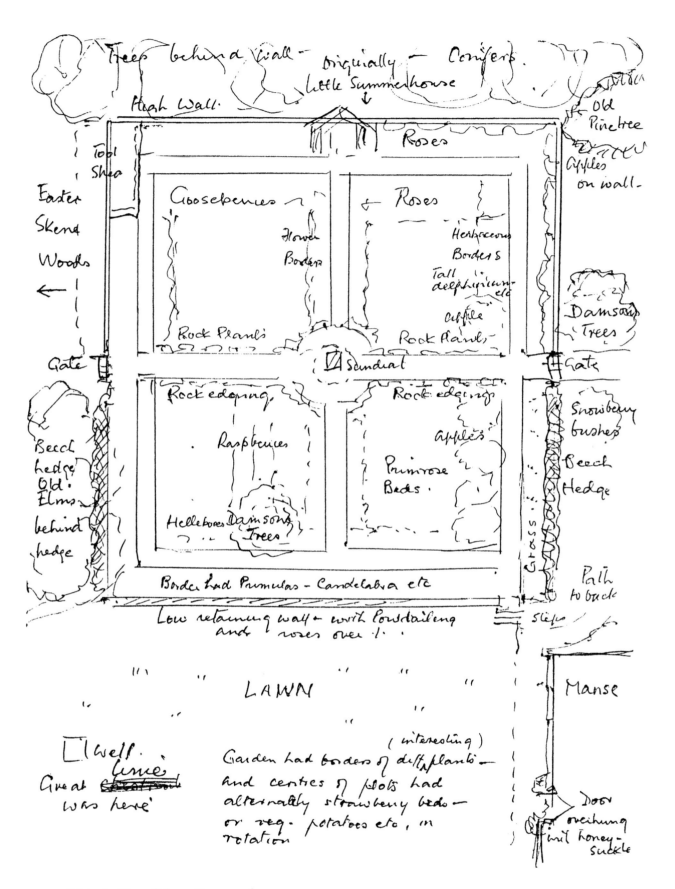

Plate 5. Plan of Skene Manse garden.

Sincere Greetings for Christmas and the New Year

Plate 6. John and Mary McMurtrie and the children – left to right, Beatrice (Bettice), Elspeth, Jean and John in the pram – Skene, 1937.

preserve the old garden flowers for a future generation.

John, who was twenty-three years older than Mary, died in 1949. She left Skene after his death and, travelling to Kenya for her daughter Jean's wedding, she painted a collection of wildflowers.

During the 1950s she became friendly with George Morrison Taylor, a great gardener whose writing is still not given the recognition it deserves (after he died his executors burned his papers, resulting in a great loss to our knowledge of gardening). Fifty years later his book *The Little Garden* remains one of the most authoritative books on how to grow the best plants and vegetables in the days before F1 hybrids meant that your own crops were all ready on the same day.

Mary and George decided to write a book on old pinks and carnations together which gave her great pleasure despite the fact that, sadly, it was never published because of George's death and the destruction of his papers. Mary never threw away her paintings of these pinks and the book that was published by the Garden Art Press in 2003, *Old Cottage Pinks*, was formed around the collection of paintings that she kept.

After John's death Mary moved to Springbank Lodge. From 1950 to 1959 the nursery gardens expanded, she had an annual plant stand at the Aberdeen horticultural shows and her success encouraged the final move to Balbithan House, Kintore, in 1960. By using the old primroses and rare native plants as a nucleus, she rapidly established a highly successful nursery which not only contributed to the restoration of the house, but was a method of distributing these plants of the previous generations. This was one of the most enterprising periods of her life, selling from the garden, catalogue sales, writing articles for the *Scots Magazine,* the *Deeside Field Club* and the *Edinburgh Tatler.*

At this time she commenced her holidays with Nan Pattullo in the Algarve (where she would return for four week visits for many years after Nan died). Winter in the Algarve with the soft beneficial effect of the gentle light also encouraged her to paint. One of her first books was the publication of a small handbook for tourists called *Wild Flowers of the Algarve.* Here, her ability to capture the light and almost make the plants move on the paper captured the enthusiasm of the University of Lisbon and in 1992, under its auspices, she illustrated *Plantas do Algarve.* Mary had helped with Nan's *Castles, Houses and Gardens of Scotland* books and a series of lectures given by Dr. Douglas Simpson on old Scottish buildings made her realise Scottish building heritage was being totally neglected. Against her solicitor's advice, she decided to restore an old laird's house. She felt the move to Balbithan was inevitable having seen its possibilities as a suitable background for the old plants she had collected over preceding years.

The difference between the climates of east and west Scotland is not generally realised. So many people in the south do not take into account the long daylight hours of summer or, indeed, the drier air of the east. (I have read that Queen Victoria bought Balmoral because she had been cruising the Western Isles in her yacht for six weeks in constant drizzle. On receiving a letter from Sir John Clark of Tillypronie – the husband of the Lady Clark whose recipes inspired Elizabeth David – complaining of the drought, she cruised round to Aberdeen to see him and decided to buy a nearby estate.)

While at Balbithan Mary restored the fortified house which dated back to the sixteenth century. She did this so successfully that after this there were few castles in the area whose owners did not consult her when they needed to carry out restoration work. At the same time she re-created the garden. Her knowledge of painting and her training as a botanical artist made her appreciate that green in its many shades was a most important colour. Here she did not use the techniques of the great landscape painters with their splashes of red; she would more frequently use pastel colours with bright scarlet almost as a full stop.

The writing had begun. There was a small early piece that she put in *The Countryman* which has always had a great influence on me as a gardener. It was headed 'Old Time Favourites' and discussed her joy in old-fashioned flowers. Cottage gardens crammed with flowers, great gardens with peaceful lawns, long borders and flowery arbours all had one thing in common – scent. It finished with a most telling paragraph:

A garden – and it can be quite a tiny garden – where old plants are treasured can be a delightful place, green and peaceful, full of soft colours and sweet scents: a garden where you can relax. It is so much more restful than one which is a blaze of colour. Even more it is a garden where you can work happily and get to know and love the plants and understand their ways: a place where there is always something to do and enjoy.

This defined her sense of a great garden and when she restored Balbithan in her unique manner she stayed with the traditional style demanded by the antiquity of the house. It was divided by straight paths, with a walk on all four sides and boundaries of yew and rose hedges. These in their turn created many smaller gardens. In spring these enclosures would be enlivened by planting some of the old named daisies now, alas, almost extinct from the Australian daisy rust. Examples of these would be the soft pink 'Alice', its crimson sport called 'Rob Roy', and the famous 'Hen and Chickens' daisy first known in gardening literature in

Parkinson's *Paradisus* in 1629 (Plate 7). These colours would be contrasted with Queen Anne's double daffodil *Narcissus* 'Eystettensis' and all would then be softened by the dark olive green leaves of *Colchicum autumnale* 'Alboplenum', which in those days was a very rare plant.

Another enclosure had alpines, pinks, dwarf campanulas and dwarf phlox. Good drainage was essential for her collection of phlox and even more so for her collection of old auriculas. Her paintings of some of these were seen by Sotheby's when they came to sell some of her husband's stamp collection and were then, with a painting of herbs, included in *The Glory of the Garden* exhibition which took place

in conjunction with the Royal Horticultural Society in 1987.

The arrangement of these plants did not rely upon any particular period, much more essentially on their charm, dotted throughout the garden. One of the joys of walking round Balbithan with Mary was the emphasis she placed on waiting for a cutting to become totally ripe before taking it. Indeed I well remember how she taught me the importance of waiting for *Hepatica triloba* pips to fill before they were detached from the main plant (Plate 9).

Despite all this activity she would still travel the local countryside recording the forms that she could find of her great love – *Rosa*

Plate 7. Hen and Chickens daisy.

Plate 8. Balbithan House, pen drawing by Mary.

spinosissima, the Scots rose (Plate 10). Pink, white and yellow, double, semi-double and single flowering, in her childhood they had been popular garden plants. She was aware that they were disappearing fast as they were being replaced by modern cultivars with their longer flowering periods. Her book on Scots roses united their fleeting beauty with the certain knowledge of their cultivation. This gave her great pleasure at the age of ninety-six when it was published by the Garden Art Press in 1998.

Fame came, slowly, like riding on a tortoise. *The Glory of the Garden* exhibition had made a larger public aware of her painting. Roy Genders asked her to illustrate his book *The Wild Flower Garden* in 1976 and, later, *Collecting Antique Plants.* When in 1982 Marc Ellington, with his Heritage Press at Towie Barclay Castle, published and had printed privately her book of *Scottish Wild Flowers,* he invited subscribers to invest in a limited edition of 750 leather-bound, gold-embossed copies. H.R.H. Princess Margaret, Countess of Snowdon, headed the list of subscribers printed in the book. The Scottish nation at large realised she was one of their first botanical painters who could be called inter-

Plate 9. *Hepatica triloba* double red.

national. The grouping of the individual flowers in her painting owes a subconscious debt to the draughtsmanship that Parkinson had used in the woodcuts in his *Paradisus* of 1629, the first truly great book on English gardening. The success of her natural style of embellishing the necessary shading to create the shadow of a living flower or plant on paper made the demand for her painting far exceed the quantity that she could hope to produce. Her books *Scots Roses, Old Cottage Pinks* and *Scottish Wild Flowers* are a lasting legacy for all who appreciate taste and elegance in the garden.

The following memories of gardening, never previously published, were written when Mary was well into her nineties.

'Old Country Gardens and their Treasures'

In the early days of the century I remember many little country gardens, cottage gardens and farm gardens, where many most interesting and unusual plants flourished – plants, I may say, that have now either vanished, or are extremely rare collectors' pieces in fact.

I remember one, a rather special garden in Garlogie, where there were double primroses, and hose-in-hose primroses with a giant form of grape hyacinth. Another garden behind a farmhouse where besides all the usual vegetables and potatoes there were large clumps of *Primula pubescens* and the more unusual lilac form. Another cottage had a little border under the house wall of flourishing hepatica – the double blue – I have never seen such splendid plants before or since. Often I have been told when I was admiring a fine double primrose or an auricula, white with powder – a real 'Dusty Miller'. That was here in my grandfather's time – it was his favourite flower.

Most gardens had a little hedge or perhaps a solitary bush of Scots roses – the commonest one I remember was double yellow; these have the most wonderful scent – the garden is filled with it when

they come into flower in June. One of my earliest recollections is of a tall bush at the gable end of our schoolhouse; I could just reach up to smell its little flowers – and behind me was the great bed of lily of the valley – where we used to gather great bunches to post to friends who lived in Edinburgh. That old garden of ours was full of scents – the old yellow day lily and the scent from the round bed with a border of the old Dusty Millers in all shades of yellow and dark brown. I had three specially loved primroses there, I can remember the exact spots where they grew – a sky blue one [a short polyanthus, I think] – a Jack in the Green primrose, very dark red nearly black and another splashed with red and white. There was also my grandfather's auricula – tall rich purple and white all over with meal. To say nothing of the gooseberry bushes which conveniently bordered every path – in at least over a dozen kinds which I do not suppose are now in existence – all delicious.

We also had at one time most of the Bon Accord primroses, when they first appeared from Cockers Nursery where they were raised – 'Gem' [Plate 11], 'Cerise', 'Purple', probably 'Lilac' and 'Lavender', and perhaps even the two lovelies 'Elegans' and 'Beauty'.

I remember Crown Imperials in another schoolhouse garden at Westhill and tall especially fine Christmas Roses later in the manse garden at Lumphanan. I do not think there were many old pinks in those early days – except the old small white and its pink variety – and probably the large double white with its pale crimson centre, so exuberant a flower it overflowed and split its calyx – later I was told it was called 'Bridal Veil'. But I do not remember the others white pink and crimson or laced – perhaps our part of Aberdeenshire was too cold and frosty.

Now it appears that the wheel has turned and so many of these old and well loved plants, for a time discarded in favour of

Plate 10. Scots. roses. *Rosa spinosissima*, the Burnet rose. 1. 'Marbled Pink'. 2. Lilac-pink (unnamed).
3. 'A', from John Innes Institute, Norwich. 4. 'Andrewsii'. 5. 'Dundee'.

Plate 11. Primrose 'Bon Accord Gem'.

newer showier flowers – have now become popular. They are being searched for but sadly many have perished. Herb gardens and herbal balms and remedies have sprung up everywhere.

Towards the end of her life she did, however, record how she had created the garden at Balbithan, almost from dereliction, but more particularly with her knowledge of the gardens and plants from the past which of course were so important to her concept of the tranquillity of a period garden with plants to match the period of the house. I have in place abridged these notes which record almost forty years of gardening.

The laying out of the present garden at Balbithan was begun when I came here in 1960. It was partly restoration and partly reconstruction. There were traditions of an early garden, but all that survived were the straight paths, typical of old Scots gardens, and some old trees, apples, yew and an ancient oak. All these were retained. A ruined wall that had divided the garden in two was rebuilt and continued on its line down the garden, but reconstruction was

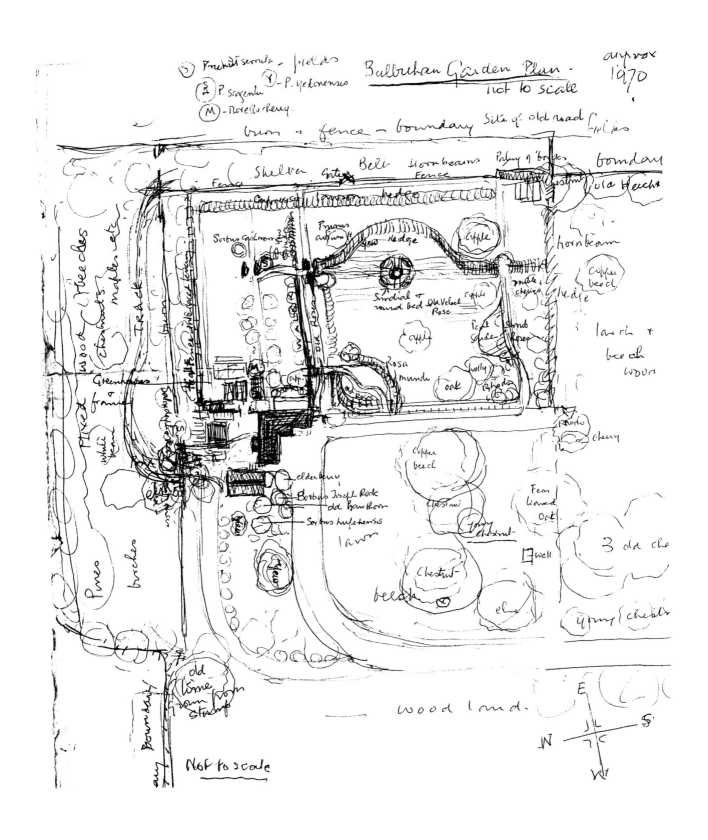

Plate 12. Balbithan House garden plan.

very gradual, and the idea of having a garden that was in keeping with the old house [part of it dated from about 1560] was never far from my mind. To this end yew hedges were planted, and one of Scots roses, another of the old striped rose *Rosa mundi*; a small bed of herbs was made and the beds laid out of old-fashioned plants and old shrub roses.

The Scots roses flower in June. There are still about eight or nine different kinds – all scented. A century ago there were far more, over a hundred named varieties, but few remain now. [All that Mary could find were eventually recorded in her book on Scots roses.] They were raised from the little single white rose of dunes and sandy river banks. The old shrub roses are at their peak about July, they have a spectacular flowering then, and the air is filled with their marvellous fragrance, but few of them have more than some sparse late flowers after this. Here in the garden there are centifolia, including some of the old favourite moss roses. Bourbon, Alba, Damask, *rugosa*, with others being added to every year. Out of interest I give a list of some that grow here. 'Alba Maxima', 'Céleste', 'Félicité Parmentier', 'Fantin-

Plate 13. Mary's eldest daughter, Beatrice (Bettice), beside the sundial at Balbithan, 1970.

Latour', 'Juno', 'Petite de Hollande', 'Blanche Moreau', 'Capitaine John Ingram', 'Comtesse de Murinais', 'Nuits de Young', 'Cardinal de Richelieu', 'La Reine Victoria', 'Louise Odier', 'Madame Pierre Oger', 'Madame Isaac Pereire', 'Souvenir de la Malmaison', 'Celsiana', 'Leda', 'Madame Hardy', 'Omar Khayyám' and 'Dupontii' [Plates 14 and 15].

There are species roses here, *Rosa moyesii* and hybrids, *Rosa rubrifolia* [Plate 16], *Rosa nitida*, *Rosa soulieana*, the well-known great climber *Rosa filipes* 'Kiftsgate' and the less well known but equally great climber *Rosa brunonii* 'Betty Sherriff' discovered by George Sherriff on his last expedition. It is a magnificent climbing rose with large trusses of beautiful, scented, single, pale pink flowers.

In the garden and around the house there are some interesting trees, *Prunus serrula* with coppery bark, the white berried *Sorbus cashmiriana*, *Sorbus* 'Joseph Rock' with yellow berries, *Syringa* x *persica*, *Syringa microphylla*, *Viburnum bodnantense* and the ancient oak. A line of double white geans [wild cherries, Plate 17] grow along the south boundary of the garden, they are a lovely sight when in flower in May.

The herb garden is quite small, but as well as marjoram, sage, balm, lavender, rue, different thymes, chives, and various mints, there are some of the herbs like elecampane.

There are a great variety of plants in the garden. In Spring the first to flower is the aconite as it pushes up through the snow. It is closely followed by snowdrops (*Galanthus*) and snowflakes (*Leucojum vernum*). Then comes a rush of little irises – *Iris histrioides* first; early species crocus, dwarf narcissus and tiny tulips. The Lenten rose *Helleborus orientalis* grows luxuriantly here in many shades as also does the larger green *Helleborus corsicus*. Daffodils and narcissus include the true *Narcissus poeticus*, the old double white daffodil, and the very

Plate 14. *Rosa x centifolia* from the garden of the Dowager Duchess of Elgin, Culross. Very finely serrated leaves, rather infolding at edges. Bud globular.

Plate 15. *Rosa* 'Cardinal de Richelieu'.

Plate 16. *Rosa glauca*, syn. *R. rubrifolia*.

Plate 17. Gean blossom.

Plate 18. *Iris histrioides* 'Major'. February 1996.

Plate 19. *Crocus tommasinianus.*

rare *Narcissus* 'Eystettensis' (Queen Anne's double daffodil). Erythroniums and a collection of different trilliums are followed by various *Meconopsis* [Plates 18-21].

Among the old-fashioned flowers now appearing are *Ranunculus aconitifolius* (Fair Maids of France), double *Lychnis* [Plate 22], Sweet Rocket (*Hesperis matronalis*), *Tradescantia*, *Hemerocallis* (the old sweet scented kind) and paeonies. There are still some double primroses, hose-in-hose and Jack in the Green. All rare now; old garden auriculas, double daisies, and a small formal garden of old pinks and lavender.

In Autumn the garden glows with colour when beds of colchicums come into flower, in all their shades of mauves and purples with the great white cups of *Colchicum speciosum* loveliest of all. [I treasure still after

Plate 20. *Trillium nivale* and *T. hibbersonii.*

Plate 21. *Trillium sessile* – white form. April 2003 (painted when Mary was 101).

Plate 22. 1. Rocket, purple and white. 2. *Mertensia*. 3. *Lychnis,* double. 4. *Geranium renardii*. 5. Heartsease.

Plate 23. Autumn crocus.

fifty years the bulbs of *Colchicum autumnale* 'Alboplenum' which she once sent me. A very rare plant then and rare still.] Nerines and *Schizostylis* then take over flowering until cut by frost, but *Viburnum bodnantense* is already in flower to bring us through the Winter and well into Spring [Plates 23 and 24].

Mary's flower painting had begun after a trip to Kenya in 1954, but most of the 1960s were concerned with redesigning the garden at Balbithan. By 1978 her success in creating the garden was being widely admired. Arthur Hellyer gave her the accolade of a feature in *Country Life* on 30 November that year. This ensured the garden's inclusion in *The*

Plate 24. *Crocus speciosus* – appears in September and October. Dark pointed buds appear and open quickly in the sun, with wide spreading petals of rich blue with a delicate tracery of darker veins. In the centre are the three bright orange-red stigmas.

Englishwoman's Garden in 1980, a book edited by Alvilde Lees-Milne and Rosemary Verey.

During the 1980s she would be accompanied on trips to the Algarve by her daughters Elspeth and Beatrice, but in the autumn she would go to France to visit Beatrice, who had married a Frenchman. At this time I was writing fairly regularly in a very learned magazine called *Historic Gardens* and an article I had written on Mary's painting and gardening was picked up by the Director of the Château de Villandry. He discussed at length with her the possibility and practicality of an exhibition of her painting, but

this did not occur because of the difficulty of transporting sufficient material.

The old pinks which had done so well in Aberdeen did not like the soil at Balbithan; they struggled, but the primroses did well. Her ability, coupled with the soil and the climate, helped her to propagate at least fifteen of the rarer double primroses maintaining her friendship further with the leading primrose growers who had commenced as the friends of her husband.

She left Balbithan in 1990 and moved to Sunhoney (Plate 26) to live with her daughter Elspeth, taking with her many of her plants.

Plate 25. Mary at Balbithan, about 1982. Photograph by Eric Ellington.

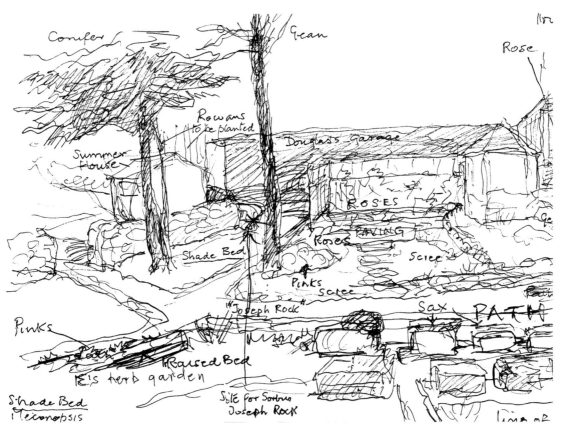

Plate 26. Plan of the garden at Sunhoney.

Chapter 2
Plant Conservation, Gardening Writers and Other Gardening Friends

In the absence of a National Society for the Preservation of Garden Plants, the nurseries run by Mary McMurtrie, Gladys Emmerson and Margery Fish were the principal suppliers of historic plants from the end of the war until the late 1970s.

Every gardener can teach us something, even if what not to do … watching plants grow. Mary's ability as a good correspondent had introduced her to a wide circle of gardening friends, although it is difficult to assess how important they were to her gardening. Of the three gardening writers discussed below, one stands out as a gardener of great importance nationally at the time. Little known, yet constantly becoming more prized for her writing and painting, Gladys Emmerson is rarely recognised as the famous Gladys Peto of before the Second World War. Indeed, Brent Elliott, Librarian of the Lindley Library, was amazed when I first sent details of her gardening. As a member of the Victorian Society he had heard of her only as an artist edging on the Bloomsbury Set.

GARDENING WRITERS

GLADYS EMMERSON

Gladys Peto was the only girl of the three children of William and Mary Jane Peto. The family centred around Cannon Court in Berkshire. Her father and Sir Harold Peto of Iford Manor were first cousins – Harold's father was Sir Samuel Morton Peto, and Gladys' grandfather was the younger brother, William. Gladys had the Peto memory – Sir Harold had designed architectural gardens, her interest was essentially practical gardening.

Born at Maidenhead, Berkshire, she studied at the local school of art from 1908 (a fellow pupil was Sir Stanley Spencer), moving to the London Society of Art in 1911. She started work as a

Plate 27. Gladys Emmerson (née Peto).

Plate 28. Merry Xmas and Happy New Year from Lindsay and Gladys, painted after a stroke partially paralysed her hand.

black and white artist, her repertoire including poster, stage and dress design (*The Times* reported it was the in thing to wear a Gladys Peto dress) and, later, pottery and furnishings. An example of her work still used in teaching advertising design is the group of children walking across a black sky enlivened by stars entitled 'The Milky Way to Health'. Allen and Hanbury's considered this their finest selling advertisement.

Her ready memory and fund of stories, limericks and anecdotes were always useful to her. At the outbreak of the First World War she wrote and illustrated a small column in the *Daily Sketch* – a national tabloid – entitled 'Letters to a Lonely Soldier', and several children's books. She showed an interest in gardens and gardening, illustrating a plate for children with the caption 'Little Patty planted peas, all in a tidy row, and every day she digs them up to notice if they grow'.

Plate 29. Snapdragon – the old Scottish striped antirrhinum – from Timothy.

In 1922 she married an army doctor, Lindsay Emmerson, following him wherever the army posted him. She wrote and illustrated travel books including a small series on Malta, Cyprus and Egypt for the *Sojourner*. Shortly before the Second World War Lindsay Emmerson was posted to Palace Barracks, Holywood, Co. Down, Northern Ireland, where they rented Stanley House from the Boyd family. Life changed when Lindsay Emmerson was posted to France and her mother, nieces and nephew joined her from England. Her planned book on

seven gardens, with the Victorian section completed, was shelved by the publisher. One of her legs had been injured in a road accident in Egypt and while running the hospital library during the war she damaged it again, falling on some ice. One leg remained smaller than the other, she had a permanent limp and could no longer dig the garden.

When the war ended they bought a smallholding called The Leeke between Limavady and Dungiven. Gladys continued her painting, confining her watercolours in those years to the Irish landscape. From The Leeke she gardened and opened her nursery to widen the distribution of the flowers that had entranced her so many years earlier when at the commencement of her children's book career she had first read *Mary's Meadow*. Aware that the days of great house gardening were passing for ever, she realised that their survival would be in the hands of smaller individual gardens. She had an immense acquaintance of local ladies who all kept one or two double cultivars of primroses in their gardens; Miss Wynne of Avoca became a future correspondent of Margery Fish.

The nursery was in the old apple orchard at The Leeke. Roy Genders, when visiting, could not help remarking on the health of the plants. In those days before sprays Gladys would constantly wash all plants on propagation and move them into fresh soil on the small nursery beds. These needed constant attention. Her god-daughter Felicity Sutton, later Lady Fisher, remembers offering to weed one of these beds only to find she had pulled up the small plants of King-in-Splendour *Betonica stachys* (*Stachys officinalis*).

Gladys advertised her plants in both *Popular* and *Amateur Gardening*. By 1958 she had twenty-one double primroses, eight Jack in the Green primroses and six hose-in-hose primroses. Many of the double primroses and Jack in the Green primroses had been supplied by John McMurtrie and, later, by Mary. She loved her rare old English flowers like the striped snapdragon (Plate 29), the double dwarf sweet william called 'King Willie' and some of the old double hepaticas also known as the snow rose, double flowering wallflowers, camomile, the perennial forget-me-not she called forget-me-never and the Great Rose Plantain of 1629 which was to figure so largely once Margery Fish planted her green garden at East Lambrook Manor. Green flowers were always an interest. I remember sending her a green auricula and the bronze leaved four leaved clover.

Eleanour Sinclair Rohde, the first scholar who had worked with early herbals, gardening and bee literature, had died in 1950. Gladys had a great sympathy with her; they had both lost brothers in the First World War. Gladys had come to terms with this; Eleanour never did. Eleanour created a small nursery which became the source of many of the plants that Mary and her friends distributed. She took in over fifty German prisoners-of-war convinced someone was doing the same for her brother in Germany. Despite having published eleven titles on historical aspects of gardening, she has never been acknowledged as the first scholar of old gardening literature who is unfailingly correct in her scholarship. Gladys was most impressed with her book on how to grow and cook uncommon vegetables, even experimenting with her recipe on how to cook sugar beet.

Gladys always regretted never having learnt Latin. She loved words and this led to her friendship with Roy Genders. He was also fascinated by primroses, writing two books on the subject. He was not so good at propagation and Gladys was frequently the source of his rarer primroses. 'Madame de Pompadour', the doyenne of all double primroses for many years, had a notoriously difficult root system and did not produce rooted offsets. Gladys and her gardener, Jack Doey, together realised that if they got the wild primroses growing well they could insert a cutting of 'Madame de Pompadour' into the root and by binding the graft they would be able to create a new plant to sell for – in those days – the vast sum of £2 each. She also did this with some of the rarer Bon Accord primroses that were losing vigour. The constant washing reduced the likelihood of vine weevil before the advent of Domestos whose 2% solution will kill all parasitic insects. This was particularly effective for *Pelargonium* cuttings where, unlike Mary McMurtrie and Margery Fish, she kept a small heated greenhouse. She enjoyed the colourful display and remembered her days in the Mediterranean and the childhood memories of her own garden.

In April 1977 Lindsay Emmerson fell carrying boxes of plants to the post. His head injuries were severe and he died a month later from double pneumonia. Gladys lost interest in life without him and died the following month.

Leaving aside her paintings and her books, her contribution to English life was the jewel-like quality of the double primroses she sent back to England – now almost all extinct. I do keep the double form of 'Wanda' that Mr. Smith of Newry found in his nursery bed and called 'Pat', only to be told he could not call it after his daughter because someone else had used the name first, so he called it 'Our Pat'. The old 'Alba Plena', 'Quaker's Bonnet' and 'Marie Crousse' still reappear, but most of the true old primroses seem gone now.

Plate 30. Margery Fish.

MARGERY FISH

Of the three ladies who kept nurseries with the principal object of ensuring the survival of the old plants, Margery Fish is the most nationally renowned. Her books, full of useful instruction, remain inspirational. Even today her *Cottage Garden Flowers* is full of those memories of waking early on a May morning, going out into the garden, hearing the thrush sing and all is well with the world. She taught you how to garden and choose the best plants. Anyone who ever put a trowel in the ground could learn from her books.

She was born Margery Townsend at Stanford Hill, London, in 1892 and educated at the Friends' School, Saffron Walden. She entered Fleet Street as Lord Northcliffe's secretary. Immensely energetic and capable, she remained at the *Daily Mail* as secretary to each successive editor until she married Walter Fish and in 1937 left London.

Together they purchased East Lambrook Manor at South Petherton for £1,000 and commenced restoring and creating the internationally famous Grade 1 listed garden that exists today. In the early stages she relied heavily on Walter's advice and followed his decisions; as time passed she grew in confidence. Walter died in 1949. As Christopher Lloyd remarked with his usual perspicacity, it was not until she was left alone that she became the popular writer and lecturer who travelled the British Isles with the sole view of ensuring the survival of the gardening heritage.

Plate 31. Carnations from Timothy July '99. 'Afton Water' and Margery Fish's double dark red (she thought the oldest).

Always conscious that a garden is a living entity, she continually experimented with new plants. At one time when I was writing the book entitled *Margery Fish's Country Gardening* I estimated there were periods when she had ten new plants in the garden every day. Her lecturing opened doors for

her. One day at the Oxford Botanic Garden she was looking over some dried specimens of pinks and saw the one that was labelled 'Bat's Double Red'. 'Would that this were available today' she sighed, as she recognised the name of a famous grower from Parkinson's *Paradisus* of 1629. 'Come into the garden', said the curator 'and I will give you some cuttings.'

This was repeated on Exmoor with the Queen of Spain daffodil. For this daffodil she retained her most evocative writing. It was first seen on the rockery of Myddelton House, Enfield, the garden of Augustus Bowles, the uncle of the Duchess of Cornwall. Margery was lecturing on Exmoor at a Women's Institute and someone had decorated her desk with the flowers. She left the village the following morning, clutching the precious bulbs. She told all her friends, she distributed them where she thought they would survive. They did not live well and gradually became fewer. David Bromley of The Moortown, Shropshire, grew them better than most. It took me some fifteen years to understand that Exmoor is an acid soil and most of us were gardening on lime. Slowly this beautiful daffodil is returning to commerce, but, a warning – imposters abound.

Primroses were probably Margery's favourite flower. She grew and named some coloured forms she considered particularly fine. These included Lambrook Yellow, Peach, Crimson and Pink. She distributed the older forms of Jack in the Green and hose-in-hose primroses and corresponded with the leading gardeners of the day. All exchanged their plants. William Chalmers of Stonehaven, Gladys Emmerson, Tony Venison and Mary McMurtrie were all recipients.

Margery was always surprised at her own fame and importance as a gardener. She had never received any formal training in gardening and to the last deferred to those who had formal degrees. She did recognise, however, that she had created a lasting memorial to her gardening by living up to the high standards that Walter had shown her when she first started gardening. The garden could never be an about-to-be or just-had-been garden. It had to be like the house, always ready for the unexpected guest. Her private rule of visiting a garden and never looking to see what she could take out of it but looking to see what she could

put in was just as important. If ever she saw what she considered to be a good garden she would ask herself back in the wintertime. I once asked the reason why and was told that in the wintertime you can see the complete bones of the garden. The plants, however we enjoy them, remain purely the decoration.

Margery Fish died on 24 March 1969. Her nephew Henry Boyd-Carpenter – now Sir Henry Boyd-Carpenter K.C.V.O. – succeeded to the property. A solicitor in London, he attempted to care for the garden but could not possibly achieve the necessary care that a garden of such ephemeral complexity needed. In 1971 his father and mother retired to East Lambrook where in fading health and declining years they maintained the Margery Fish Trust. By 1979 the death of Francis Boyd-Carpenter gave visiting gardeners cause for concern. Although I live in Cambridgeshire, my cousin, Hazelmary Lyon (whose exploits as an early aviator and parachutist are recorded in *Blackwood's Magazine* as Wendy – the only woman on the course), lived in Devon. We had always been close, and I visited her regularly. On one journey I remember calling at East Lambrook and seeing a plant of the semi-double primrose 'Red Paddy' falling out of the ground. This would have caused Margery distress. I told Tony Venison, at that time the Gardening Editor of *Country Life*, who took immediate action. He allowed me to write an article on her life and gardening which was to appear simultaneously with the advertisement of the house. This coincided with the efforts of the Somerset Branch of the National Society for the Preservation of Garden Plants to have the garden listed and a purchaser for the property quickly found. Although house and garden have changed hands since then, great efforts have been made to ensure that the very essence of one of our greatest gardeners since Gertrude Jekyll has been kept alive and not preserved in aspic to become a museum without a memory.

From: Mrs. MARGERY FISH.

EAST LAMBROOK MANOR,
SOUTH PETHERTON, SOM.

Tel.: South Petherton 328.

1 Feb 1960.

Dear Mrs McMurtrie,

Thank you very much for your letter – It is most thrilling to hear of your new house. I am sure you will make it all lovely and I hope I shall get up to Aberdeen one of these days to see you in your new surroundings. I am always glad we managed to get to see you the last time I was in Scotland –

Let me know, when you are ready, if there are any old plants I can send you. I collect herbs, among other things, and any old plants I can get hold of.

At the moment I am trying to find all the old cottage chrysanthemums I can. There used to be a lot of them. They were treated like any other perennial plant and were easy and pleasant.

Don't worry about the double white primroses because I have promises of them from two sources. Mine felt the heat but most of the others are magnificent & I have quite good stocks of lilacina plena, Bon Accord, M. Crousse, Old rose, etc. My best wishes for the new venture.

Yours sincerely Margery Fish.

Plate 32. Letter from Margery Fish to Mary McMurtrie.

Plate 33. Timothy Clark with 'Abraham', a Dark Cuckoo Maran cockerel from a Cumbrian animal sanctuary whose progeny have won many prizes.

TIMOTHY CLARK

My great-grandmother came from a family of some repute with a female connection to Oliver Cromwell whose family had come back to the Fens after they fell from power. She lost all her money in the cattle plague of 1845 and then helped the people of Wicken, Cambridgeshire, with a Culpeper's herbal. I do not think she ever cured anyone, but in those days with no doctor in the village she did at least sell bottles of hope. My grandmother and aunt kept the plants and I commenced gardening at an early age. When I was seven I was sent to the King's School at Ely where Roy Genders taught me Latin and first introduced me to Mrs. Emmerson. If I had been a doctor I would never have been a gardener. The interest then and always remains to make a sick plant better.

My cousin Hazelmary Lyon first flew at the Hendon Airshow in 1919. We were very close

friends and as I was growing up one day she said to me that when I was old life would be difficult because most of the friends that she had learned to fly with had been killed in the Battle of Britain or over Berlin. There would be no one to speak for us. This made me aware that the world I knew was disappearing. Her father wrote copperplate with a fine hand; every afternoon when I was eight he would allow me to write one sentence in a book he had created to show me the importance of clear writing.

I had always had an interest in my grandmother's plants and began to correspond with most of the people mentioned above. We were all involved in exchanging plants, many of which we realised were represented by only twenty or thirty cultivars. I worked in the family business for many years and in 1961 had the opportunity to commence writing the leading article on commodities for the *London Corn Circular* whose editor at the time was Philip Sidey (he later moved on to create Pebble Mill, the television programme). I wrote this column fairly regularly until 1973. I had joined the Garden History Society and written on Mrs. C.W. Earle *(Pot Pourri from a Surrey Garden)*. Penelope Hobhouse, having read this, asked me to write up for the *Journal* the tour of Tuscan gardens she organised in 1978. Tony Venison, the then editor of gardening for *Country Life,* read it and asked to see anything else I might write on gardening. As a result I have written on various plants and people I have known since 1980 in *Country Life* and *The Garden*. He also suggested I join the Historic Houses Association who he considered would be of great help in preserving the plant heritage.

Mary and I commenced our correspondence in the mid-1960s, principally about plants. Jessica, my second daughter, died in 1966 and at that time I sent my primroses to a friend of Mary's called Cecil Monson in Ireland. She wrote me a very understanding letter when she heard of this and subsequently we tended to write more on family and gardening. The letters would increase in frequency if we were undergoing a family crisis but rarely return to the reason why we were writing.

Plate 34. *Hesperis* – Rocket – Dames Violet – double white, very rare. Sent by Timothy Clark, July 1999.

I also bred Dark Cuckoo Maran chickens during these past fifty years (Plate 33). We never arranged a marriage between the chickens which now I greatly regret.

Of the many plants I have saved from extinction the most interesting was probably the double flowering sweet rocket (Plate 34). I always thought I had this from Margery Fish, but when I wrote the book on her gardening I was surprised to find a letter from her saying I had offered it to her. Fashions in gardening come and go, but with so little interest in our history I frequently find that the plants that I keep are becoming rare survivors. I do not understand this. These plants take up little space and, as gardens become smaller, I would have thought that they would be ideal for the smaller modern house rather than decking and grasses.

OTHER GARDENING FRIENDS

Plate 35. David Bromley and Mary at The Moortown, August 1993.

David Bromley and Mary originally became acquainted through corresponding about double primroses. They were good friends for many years – indeed David would frequently join Mary and Elspeth to paint in the Algarve. His interest in snowdrops led him to becoming one of the first collectors of their cultivars and species and his interest in old garden plants has helped him to achieve a very memorable garden at The Moortown in Shropshire (usually open to the public under the National Garden Scheme). He was almost certainly the preserver of the true Queen of Spain daffodil. His memory for a good plant is remarkable; only in 2007 he asked me to give him some of the crimson black *Chrysanthemum* 'Venus' which had been given to my father-in-law by one of the Professors at Cambridge University when he worked at The Old Schools. He was delighted to receive it with the Plymouth strawberry which was found by a woman picking strawberries in a wood near Plymouth, probably around 1550 because it was mentioned in Gerard (1598) and Parkinson

(1629) and would have needed time to be distributed. Unique because it had leaves instead of seeds, it was greatly admired and was depicted in paintings as a jewel.

David shared with Mary an interest in old roses and pinks, at one time collecting many species. Some of these he passed to Mary who recorded them in her book *Old Cottage Pinks*.

The Logan-Home sisters lived at Silverwells, Edrom, and ran a very successful alpine nursery. They were almost the same age as Mary and the three became close friends. Mollie and Edith were charming and excellent company and looked on Mary as 'their little sister'.

Their knowledge of growing smaller alpine plants was quite exceptional at the time. They travelled widely, gaining a reputation as plant hunters and collectors in both China and the Himalayas, and belonged to the group who were constantly exchanging plants with each other. Hepaticas and primroses tended to overlap with Mary's knowledge. Mary always preferred the older plants that carried with them a sense of history so consequently there was a limit to their

Plate 36. From David Bromley's garden.

Plate 37. Mollie and Edith Logan-Home at Silverwells, Edrom, about 1953.

Plate 38. Mollie Harbord and Mary in the garden at Springbank Lodge, 1950s.

plant sharing. I could never understand Mary's interest in *Aquilegia viridiflora* – she was very proud of having been its only grower at one time – and I have concluded that it is possibly a plant that Mollie and Edith were growing in the nursery which for some reason had a crop failure and Mary was able to return it to them.

All three were always closely involved with **Mollie Harbord** of St. Andrews and later Loch Carron. Mollie Harbord's knowledge of gardening was immense and she later worked as a professional gardener with General Murray-Lyon in Perthshire.

Alex Duguid, who worked with the Edrom nursery, was a considerable influence. He was able to undertake the heavy work of exhibiting at the R.H.S. shows in London. His skill in propagating and raising plants was well known and he received seed from plant collectors and expeditions. When Mollie and Edith died and Silverwells was sold, they left him the nursery which he moved across the road. This continued for a few years until he retired and moved to Ballater. This was nearer to the entire

McMurtrie family and the friendship continued until his death.

Gardeners from all backgrounds enjoy talking about their plants and those of their friends almost as much as seeing and growing them. Meetings with two friends who lived locally, **Mrs. Irene Mackie** (an art school contemporary of Mary's daughter, Elspeth) and **Dr. Gordon Smith**, a botanist, satisfied this need frequently. Both were interested in old roses and Mrs. Mackie collected and grew old Scots roses from old houses and gardens. Some of these are illustrated in *Scots Roses*. As the inveterate collector of interesting garden plants as well as bizarre ferns, Mrs. Mackie had much to talk about and progress round the Mackie garden was very slow, but very rewarding. Little escaped the eagle eyes of two artists.

Dr. Smith was also interested in the native flora and progress on car trips into the Aberdeenshire countryside involved many stops and gentle walks. There were even some searches done in reverse gear so as not to miss something glimpsed at speed! Roadside verges,

Plate 39. Alex Duguid, Jean Gardner (Mary's daughter) and Mary at Balbithan, 1986.

field margins and patches of woodland were all very much appreciated in an intensively farmed landscape. Wild flowers and fruit provided a rich harvest and can be seen in many paintings, cards and books such as *Scottish Wild Flowers*. Horses also necessitated stops as Mary had been keen on drawing them earlier in life.

With another local friend, **John Aitken**, the favourite topic was alpines. His 'Great Wall of China', a double drystone wall filled with rubble and grit, encouraged the flowering of many small bulbs and difficult to grow alpines. At Balbithan a similar but rounded structure was stuffed with pinks, grey-leaved plants and auriculas. Who had the original idea we do not know. John Aitken's large greenhouse collection of florists' auriculas was a delight each spring and together they exchanged plants. (Mary's painting of 'Mrs. Cairns' Blue' auricula is in my opinion the loveliest and most evocative painting that she ever achieved.) Both were frequent exhibitors at Scottish Rock Garden Club shows in Aberdeen in the 1960s, with Mary selling plants and paintings.

Plate 40. Auricula 'Mrs. Cairns' Blue'.

45

CHAPTER 3
Aconites, Hacquetia, Hepaticas and Snowdrops

Plate 41. Snowdrops and aconites.

It is not generally appreciated in the British Isles how long the winters can be once north of Edinburgh. Mary waited for the spring, not only for the lengthening days, but also for the joy which the early flowers brought to her. One of the most interesting drawings that she did in 1988 was of aconites and snowdrops; she grouped them coming out of the ground together. This was a combination that she continually enjoyed with the contrast of gold and silver, early in the year, the two colours complementing each other, the shadows created making the grouping more successful.

The aconite has a long history in our gardens. It has always been reputed to have been poisonous and rabbits and cattle do not

Plate 42. Aconites, snowdrops, primroses, white periwinkle.

Plate 43. *Hacquetia epipactis.*

graze where it has been grown. I believe, however, that much of the fear of it comes from the name which is allied to *Aconitum*. This was the poison that reputedly gave Jason so much difficulty; on being offered it by Medea, he threw it to the ground and the marble it fell upon cracked. The problem of its nomenclature persisted through the centuries. The current name is *Eranthis hyemalis* and, like the hellebore, it belongs to the buttercup family, Ranunculaceae. The name of winter wolf's bane was used by John Gerard in 1597 when he recorded it in his *Herball* or *Historie of Plantes,* the name used by Parkinson when he recorded it in his *Paradisus* in 1629. The early botanists were never clear as to the correct name and in

the mid-eighteenth century 'Sir' John Hill set it into a separate family he called Cammarium, after an unidentified plant of the *Ranunculus* family mentioned by the first century Greek scientist Dioscorides. Its present name means flower of the earth, but even here scholars disagree, some saying that it is er=spring and anthos=flower. Earth flower does seem more appropriate, as it hugs the ground rarely growing more than five or six centimetres (two or two and a half inches) high.

Hacquetia was another of the small early flowering plants that Mary used in the rock garden to add interest. Like all good plants, it has suffered from the botanists. At one time it was called *Dondia epipactus*, but now is better known as *Hacquetia*. The name comes from Balthasar Hacquet (1740-1815), the author of *Plantae Alpinae Carniolicae*. As early as 1659 Sir Thomas Hanmer wrote of it in his *Gardening Book* as the yellow hepatica. Mary always described it as charming and unusual, but in the case of Eleanour Sinclair Rohde, whose opinion was greatly admired, particularly by Margery Fish, it was a green flowered gem whose flowers, with petals like green bracts in a whorl round the minute umbels of yellow blooms in the centre, appear first, with leaves of a peculiar colour and three lobed. A slow growing plant who resents disturbance, it likes a rather moist spot and plenty of leaf mould. Given these conditions it will increase and occasionally produce seedlings. One of these seedlings called 'Thor Svantisson' has silver edged leaves of the most impressive grey green like the colour of a 'Princess Alexandra' *Pelargonium*. It is an unusual and highly decorative plant which I with my lack of water am always prepared to try to increase by never letting it dry out at the root. The flowers are scentless but in a room develop a delicious fragrance.

It was with hepaticas Mary showed a skill few people have ever equalled. *Hepatica triloba* (see page 15) is a plant of the northern hemisphere, first mentioned in the *Feate of Gardening* (1440). The Dutch realised its use in decorating the parterre. In 1614 Crispin van der Passe illustrated it in his *Hortus Floridus* and it is mentioned in both Gerard 1597 and Parkinson 1629. Samuel Gilbert in his *Florists Vade-Mecum* of 1682 records

These are the prettiest flowers of the spring
Clothed in red-white and ultramarine
mantling.

It was widely used in early herbal medicine because the shape of the leaves was considered to be the same as a liver – hence its popular name of liverwort. The single flowering form is usually a good clear Prussian blue, with the occasional white variant. Its introduction to our gardens is well recorded in all the early literature. Propagation, however, is difficult. The single forms produce seed which needs about three years to grow to flowering size. The double flowering forms have to be propagated vegetatively. The usual advice given is to remove the clump from the soil and split it up carefully with between three and five pips to the clump. Mary would wait until late May or early June and then gently tease from the original plant one pip with as much root as possible attached to it. It would then be planted and in three years' time it would be a flowering size clump. I have observed that it takes this time for any hepatica to settle down.

George Morrison Taylor remembered the double blue form from his childhood. He obtained a source of it in Denmark and then distributed it among his friends. This was the source that John McMurtrie drew on, and for many years the principal source of this rare plant was Mary or her friend David Chalmers at the Blackbutts Nursery in Stonehaven nearby. They never obtained the double flowering white form although it has recently been imported from Japan and the Czech Republic and is proving as easy to grow as the double flowering red form. In Mary's catalogue the double blue was 10s.6d. but the double flowering red in 1972 was only 3s. at a time when most ordinary garden plants in her catalogue cost 2s.6d. I always remember the kindness of Gladys Emmerson when she first sent me a clump of the double red to point out that the roots of the hepatica are particularly fibrous; they must never be exposed too long to the air.

The accepted method of growing European hepaticas is on a well-drained chalk loam. In my opinion they like their roots in this soil but to receive a generous top dressing of leaf mould each autumn to stop them growing out of the ground. I have observed that this is the treatment that they receive in the forests of Northern Europe. This gives them the added bonus that when in growth in English gardens they are, like lily of the valley (*Convallaria*), able to accommodate dry shade.

Plate 44. 1. *Anemone nemorosa,* double white. 2. *A. nemorosa* 'Blue Bonnet', single, coloured. 3. *A. nemorosa* 'Robinsoniana'. 4. *Hepatica* double red, single and double blue. 5. Old pink primrose.

In view of the length of our correspondence it continually surprises me that Mary did not succumb to galanthomania – a term which Tony Venison always used for gardens so full of slightly differing types of snowdrop that frequently the only way to tell the cultivars apart was to look at the label. David Bromley of The Moortown, Shropshire, had a collection of several hundred different named varieties and Mary was always delighted to receive some of these. I have continually tried to keep the numbers of varieties under control in my garden, because a garden can become crowded with one species to the exclusion of a wider range of plants. We did have quite a long correspondence over the various forms of yellow snowdrops.

In my childhood, when Roy Genders was teaching me Latin, Canon Boughey had his wife's relations Brigadier and Mrs. Mathias and their children living at the Vicarage for the duration of the war. I remember waiting to catch the bus to Ely and noticing the snowdrops that were planted by the Grammar School. I was later told that these snowdrops, forms of *Galanthus elwesii,* had been the subject of correspondence in *The Times* before the war. They grew at the Vicarage. After the war the Mathias family moved to the home of Walter Butt, Hyde Hall in Gloucestershire, where quite by chance once they cleared the brambles and nettles they were rewarded with a garden full of rare and interesting forms of snowdrop. Three times their daughter Armine appeared in my life. First when I was a child, secondly when my daughter was at St. Mary's Convent in Cambridge and Sister Denis, as Armine then was called, cared for her. The third time was when I wrote the book on Margery Fish who had been a friend of the Mathias family when they started the Giant Snowdrop Company. It was then I realised what an important part in the history of snowdrop growing the Soham cultivar of *Galanthus elwesii* had been. Consequently I have now named it Brigadier Mathias to record its importance and given it to interested gardeners.

Plate 45. Yellow snowdrops.

At some point during the 1960s someone gave me a double yellow snowdrop quite distinct from 'Lady Elphinstone' (see Plate 47, right). I grew it, but because it was not considered exceptional by the experts I did not bother to propagate it. However during the mid-'90s I gave some to growers in the West Country. They realised its true worth. I wrote to Mary asking if it had crossed her path. She became interested in the yellow snowdrops and grew them to record their variations. Over the years I had experimented with growing the seed of *Galanthus lutescens* in its single form. One of

these seedlings was so good that Matthew Bishop, whose monograph is the standard work on Snowdrop variants, called it 'Netherhall Yellow'. For some thirty years I had been giving the double form away as 'Netherhall Yellow' so that both single and double forms now appear in commerce (Plate 47, left).

Mary added different varieties to the garden without consciously collecting them. In 1860 there was only the wild *Galanthus nivalis* grown in our gardens but by 1880, following the introduction of *G. plicatus* after the Crimean War, *G. elwesii* had been introduced along with *G. nivalis* subsp. *imperati*, a fine form the late Mr. James Atkins of Painswick procured from the kingdom of Naples. In 1875 Lord Walsingham, when travelling in Albania, collected some bulbs and sent them to the Reverend Henry Harpur Crewe. They included a snowdrop which flowered in October; this was the beginning of the snowdrop season extending from October through until April. Subsequently, of course, various cultivars were added. I remember once sending Mary 'Sam Arnott', a finely scented cultivar with a pervading honey scent named after a former Provost of Dumfries. The yellow form called 'Lutescens' (Plate 47, above) was discovered by Mr. Sanders of Cambridge in an old Northumberland garden in the 1880s; collectively these have been the source of the material which has given such a plethora of varieties today.

In conclusion I believe the reason that Mary did not collect snowdrops was because she felt rather as Margery Fish did over primroses, that they were being bred so that the original forms were becoming lost in their plethora of names – real effort was needed to distinguish many of them without the help of their label. However, as she was essentially an artist who enjoyed recording the seasons, whenever she was given a distinct snowdrop she invariably planted it in the garden, sometimes to paint, but just as usually to enjoy.

Plate 46. Double yellow snowdrop.

Plate 47. Above. *Galanthus nivalis* Sandersii Group (syn. *G. lutescens*). Left. *Galanthus* 'Netherhall Yellow'. Right. *Galanthus nivalis* 'Lady Elphinstone'.

CHAPTER 4
Daffodils

Mary and I were never gripped with a great desire to create a collection of daffodils. There were, however, one or two that were so curiously beautiful in their manner that she could not help recording them. For example, 'Rip van Winkle', with his almost dandelion flowers in March, and the old Vincent 'Van Sion' (Plate 48), a form of the wild double daffodil, were easily grown. Not so easy was Queen Anne's double daffodil (*N.* 'Eystettensis'), but George Morrison Taylor had always considered it a great favourite and consequently we both of us treated it with care. It has always surprised me that Queen Anne furniture can be priced in thousands of pounds but Queen Anne's double daffodil is merely worth five. It was Queen Anne of Austria and not our Queen Anne who gave it her name (Plate 49).

'Argent', with its curiously coloured petals in pale and dark yellow, was another hybrid and the double white form of *Narcissus cernuus* remained a great favourite. We could neither of us understand why the daffodil which had inspired so many poets over the centuries had lost its capacity to dream. For example,

> Daffodils that come before the swallow dares
> And take the winds of March with beauty
> > William Shakespeare

> The daffodils are by the curious
> Whether legitimate or spurious
> Accounted beauties in their time
> Deserving notice in our rhime
> > Samuel Gilbert, *The Florists
> > Vade-Mecum*, 1682

Plate 48. Old double daffodil 'Van Sion'.

Plate 49. 1. *Erysimum cheiri* – 'Harpur Crewe' – an old double wallflower – Rev. Henry Harpur Crewe, rector of Drayton Beauchamp. 2. Narcissus – double – 'Butter and Eggs'. 3. Narcissus – double – 'Van Sion' (old double daffodil, often greenish). 4. *Narcissus* 'Eystettensis' – 'Queen Anne's Daffodil' – Anne of Austria. 5. *Narcissus minor* – Lent lilies.

Plate 50. The old green daffodil.

I wandered lonely as a cloud
That floats on high o'er vale s and hills,
When all at once I saw a crowd,
A host of golden daffodils
                    William Wordsworth.

Why are there no poets writing about daffodils today?

In 1884 Peter Barr organised a great daffodil conference. Its object was to record the hybridising that the Hon. and Reverend Dean Herbert (1840), Edward Leeds and William Backhouse, amongst others, had achieved. It was to be the first attempt to name and classify the various hybrids with their conflicting nomenclature. These hybrids increased in number and size until the outbreak of the First World War. After this they were superseded by the larger daffodil with stronger colours, stiffer flowers and greater increase of bulb than had ever been previously known.

John Parkinson in his *Paradisi in Sole Paradisus*

Terrestris (1629) enumerates the daffodils that would set seed. He records the first evidence of a garden seedling, the double flowering Spanish daffodil. 'I thinke none ever had this kind before myself, nor did I myself ever see it before the year 1618, for it is mine owne raising and flowering first in mine owne garden'. Parkinson's Great Rose daffodil *(N. pseudonarcissus flore pleno* var.) is widely naturalised in parkland today.

Both John Evelyn in his *Calendarium Hortense* (1671) and later *Miller's Gardener's Dictionary* record saving seed and growing the seedlings to flowering. The Hof van Eden in Utrecht have the records and bulbs of some twenty hybrids from the eighteenth century that a local nobleman had grown from seed. A plate in the Lindley Library of Edwards' *Botanical Register* shows six cultivars that the Hon. and Reverend Dean Herbert had produced. He did this because he was of the opinion, indeed suspicious, that many of the so called species of his day were in actual fact natural hybrids. He proved this with such success that the Reverend George Engleheart repeated it to prove to his satisfaction that *incomparibilis*, x *odorus*, *gracilis* and x *johnstonii* amongst others were indeed natural hybrids. In passing, both the Hon. and Reverend Dean Herbert and his relative the Reverend George Herbert Engleheart were known as poets in their day, but none of their poems has given the eclectic arts as much pleasure as the daffodils they created. Few daffodils today make the impact that 'Beersheba', the first white of good constitution, made in its day. Forty years later Margery Fish was still commenting that it was the best daffodil she knew whose colouring would show so well against old oak panelling.

When Margery Fish published *Cottage Garden Flowers* in 1961 she wrote:

The daffodils that grew in the old gardens are not those we usually buy today. With all the new varieties to tempt us it is difficult not to fill the spring garden with fresh types, and most of us succumb to a few new varieties every year. The cottagers are more loyal. In their gardens the old friends come up every year and it never occurs to the owners to oust them, nor to lift and divide them. They increase, of course but they do not seem to deteriorate.

She was making a most percipient remark. Daffodils were changing and not necessarily for the better. She had already said that if breeders continued altering primroses the way they were they would soon be unrecognisable as the garden flower we knew. Her comments on daffodils made me all the more determined to save as many of the old double flowering and the rarer single flowering daffodils as I could accommodate. Now that the interest in old daffodils is becoming almost a cult, similar to snowdrops, great interest is aroused in how I display and keep them. Sally Kington, the now retired registrar of daffodils at the R.H.S., on first seeing them remarked to me she would have to reappraise her opinion of Margery Fish.

The forms of daffodil that Mary was familiar with, and enjoyed, were the old double daffodil of 'Van Sion', the single wild daffodil, early hybrids and natural variations like 'Princeps', 'Emperor' and 'Empress', and double flowering forms with old English names like 'Codlins and Cream' or 'Butter and Eggs' where the petals were mixed in varying shades of yellow and cream. However, as we all became aware in the seventies and eighties of the loss to the gardening heritage of so many old cultivars, it remained essential that no plant was ever taken into her garden just because it was old. It had to be a good plant in its own right. A particular instance of this was the variety called 'Argent' which was a cross between Parkinson's double daffodil and *Narcissus ornatus* produced in 1902. Twenty-five years later Ernest Augustus Bowles wrote, not quite accurately, 'this has grown in our gardens for over a century and it is still one of the best'.

What went wrong that the daffodils no longer inspired the sort of poetry that would

Plate 51. *Narcissus scabulerus* 'Segovia' from Irene Mackie.

resonate round the world, which even had a species called the Poet's narcissus? Tastes change, but it does appear perfection of form and instant blazing colour do not inspire the elegant planting that took place at the end of the century. When I was writing my first column on commodities Philip Sidey, my editor, insisted never pose a rhetorical question without an answer. Here is my belief – and I am sure Mary would agree: the early daffodils were not quite perfect. For many years I have grown some thousand florist tulip bulbs to return the progeny to the Wakefield Society. Every year I am amazed at the selection of individual colours that each cultivar will produce and rarely a perfect flower. Nothing like this happens in modern daffodils; one look and you are finished. The triumph of art over nature which Mary always tried to achieve in her painting and gardening does not seem to flourish in the modern daffodils today.

Plate 52. 1. Solomon's Seal. 2. Pheasant's Eye narcissus. 3. Old double white narcissus. 4. Lily of the valley. 5. Woodruff. 6. Star of Bethlehem.

CHAPTER 5
Primroses and Auriculas

PRIMROSES

Benjamin Disraeli was an influential writer on the old plants which interested Mary. His book *Lothair* led the opinion of garden writers in the period 1870-1890, as carpet bedding became less fashionable. His description of Corisande's garden aptly sums up the interest in the charm of the old world garden

'How I hate modern gardens!' said St

Aldegonde. 'What a horrid thing this is! Give me cabbage roses, sweet peas and wallflowers. That is my idea of a garden. Corisande's garden is the only sensible thing of the sort'. . . . as they entered it now, it seemed a blaze of roses and carnations, though one recognised in a moment the presence of the lily, the heliotrope, and the stock. Some white peacocks were basking on the southern wall.

Plate 53. *Primula vulgaris.*

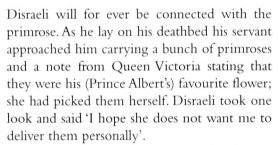

Plate 54. *Primula* hose-in-hose.

Plate 55. *Primula* double Jack in the Green and hose-in-hose.

Disraeli will for ever be connected with the primrose. As he lay on his deathbed his servant approached him carrying a bunch of primroses and a note from Queen Victoria stating that they were his (Prince Albert's) favourite flower; she had picked them herself. Disraeli took one look and said 'I hope she does not want me to deliver them personally'.

Juliana Ewing's story of *Mary's Meadow,* inspired by William Morris and the Arts and Crafts movement, was a scion of the trend away from carpet bedding and sub-tropical gardening (she was connected by marriage to some of the intellectual gardeners of the day), but that was dealing with a hose-in-hose cowslip. The cult of the double primrose came because they were quite simply beautiful, fleeting and capricious. If you were one of the fortunate ones who could grow them then you could exchange them for any plant that you wished to grow.

John McMurtrie had commenced his collection during the 1930s and his correspondence with Eda Hume shows that even then there were problems with their propagation. I have observed that all of the old primroses are best propagated in September, putting them into J. Arthur Bowers seed and potting compost and cold framed throughout the winter. The propagation should be done with a sharp knife cutting the carrot just below where the new roots are emerging. It is worthwhile to then plant the carrot as it will on occasion throw up a new set of shoots. Never let the plants get small; it is easier to propagate from a large growing plant than from one that is getting smaller.

The primrose and the cowslip can justly claim to be among the first of all English garden flowers, and none more so than the hose-in-hose, for it has to be remembered that they came to cultivation long before the influx of plants from the New World. Here, where I am fortunate if there are twenty inches (fifty centimetres) of rain a year, I have created a strain of the old primroses from seed. These

Plate 56. *Primula vulgaris* 'Lilacina Plena'.

throw hose-in-hose, Jack in the Green, Jackanapes on Horseback and once or twice a double flowering Jack in the Green. They have grown by survival of the fittest over many generations.

Margery Fish, Roy Genders and Mary herself have written with such knowledge on growing double primroses I feel that I can only add that I harvest the seed of my strain of Tudor style primroses when ripe in June. I then refrigerate it. In mid-October, once the cooler nights arrive, I plant the seeds in a good compost which must be weed free, give them a good watering (water temperature about 100 degrees Fahrenheit or 38 degrees Centigrade), place the seed boxes in a cold frame and check them for slug damage during the winter. In early April I plant them out into their flowering position because, if established, they will make full use of the dew in early May to

Plate 57. *Primula elatior* 'Derncleughi', old rare double polyanthus (form of double gold laced).

Plate 58. Double primrose 'Marie Crousse'.

withstand the later summer drought. By giving them eighteen months before flowering the plants are then in full bloom the following Easter. When Mary moved to Sunhoney we did consider whether she would get more enjoyment from them than from the old cultivars. In the end she decided that she would rather remain with the older ones, both for the continuity of her painting and to conserve the older varieties.

Gold and silver laced polyanthus have equally been reproduced from seed with more success than was common in the 1930s. It is my opinion that primroses and polyanthus are perennial, but not long lived, and consequently have to be regrown from seed every twenty or thirty years. The long lived ones are the sports which have occurred from the wild, like double yellow and white and 'Quaker's Bonnet' which in pale lilac must surely be one of the loveliest flowers ever grown. When Andrew Norton moved to East Lambrook Manor, Margery Fish's garden, I gave him a plant of primrose which I always called 'Not Belvedere'. Tony Venison had found it in a ditch in Cambridgeshire. Barbara Shaw, who was illustrating a book on primroses, decided

Plate 59. Gold laced polyanthus. This is one of the older seedlings. Nowadays, with the Barnhaven seed strains, the flowers in the garden centres are considerably larger.

that this was definitely the parent of the elusive 'Quaker's Bonnet'.

There was a time in the 1950s when Margery Fish and many of the leading primrose growers decided that it should be possible to propagate the Jack in the Green primrose by layering it as one would a carnation. I never remember anyone succeeding in this. I know I wasted a considerable amount of time and too much rainwater and never succeeded. We all enjoyed writing to each other about our failures.

Interest in old primroses did not stop with the double flowering and the Parkinson variations. There was increasing interest in growing the single flowering forms, which showed colour differences. Roy Genders, Margery Fish and Helen Champernowne in Devon were all breeding interesting plants by the addition of the blood of *Primula* 'Wanda' to the native primrose. It was the 'Garryarde' strain from Ireland with their dark bronze leaves which attracted most attention in commerce. Today (Garryarde) 'Guinevere' is still seen occasionally in the garden centres. When the nursery was at its most active there were seven Garryarde cultivars constantly sold, and Mary's private collection contained a further five. These were well bred; even today the strength of the clear orange of 'Garryarde Enchantress' still shows through in my seedling strain of the Parkinson primroses.

Mary enjoyed these single forms which she listed as modern *juliae* primroses. Some of these, of course, like the one called 'Bird of Paradise' with its mixture of colours, became the stuff of legend because of the difficulty in keeping it propagated, while others like 'Blue Riband', 'Craddock White' and 'Kinlough Beauty' remain in commerce today. Two particular favourites were 'MacWatt's Cream' and 'MacWatt's Claret' (Plates 60 and 61), both of which can still be bought. 'Macwatt's Claret' had a challenge in capturing the burgundy moving to purple and was regularly painted for this reason. The last word, however, must go to John Rea in his *Flora, Ceres and Pomona* (1646):

The common double primrose is so well known that it is sufficient only to name it, but were it not so common in every Countrywoman's Garden, it would be more respected, for indeed it is a sweet and dainty double flower, and the chiefest of all our English Kindes.'

Plate 60. *Primula* 'MacWatt's Cream'.

Plate 61. *Primula* 'MacWatt's Claret'.

Plate 62. Modern double primroses including 1. 'Ken Dearman', 2. 'Ethell Dell' (possibly), 3. 'Corporal Baxter', 4. 'Miss Indigo', 5. 'Sue Jervis', 6. 'Eugenie', 7. 'Dawn Ansell' (possibly), 8. 'Rhapsody' and 9. 'Val Horncastle'.

Plate 63. Garden auricula 'Old Purple Dusty Miller' – the long stalks are typical. I think it is the tallest of the Dusty Millers and the hardiest.

AURICULAS

Primula auricula was another flower which made the gardening and painting that Mary did better known to the outside world. *The Glory of the Garden* exhibition at Sotheby's in 1987 contained two of her paintings. The one depicting single auricula flowers was marked by the clarity of its simplicity. Other painters tended to paint whole heads of flower but here Mary took one individual pip from the head of the flower .This gained the following praise from Dr. Gordon Smith: 'no fiddly detail, no hard edges but a complete evocation of what an auricula is – grey and mealy, soft yet with substance and crowned by bright clear eyes of colour'.

The show auricula, with its florist forms and standards, was a plant of great historical interest.

Plate 64. Old garden auriculas. 1. 'Pale Yellow Old Dusty Miller.' 2. 'Rufus.' 3. 'Old Lilac Dusty Miller.' 4. 'Mrs. Cairns' Old Blue.' 5. 'Old Wine Dusty Miller.' 6. 'Old Purple Dusty Miller.' 7. 'Old Suffolk Bronze.' 8. Modern seedling. 9. 'Craig Dhu', a very old variety. 10. 'Old Crimson–black Dusty Miller'. 11. 'Old Cinnamon Dusty Miller'. 12. 'Old Red Dusty Miller'. 13. 'Old Yellow Dusty Miller Straloch'.

Plate 65. Garden auricula 'Old Cinnamon Dusty Miller'.

The climate and the style of gardening that Mary undertook did not suit the care that they needed. Her interest in auriculas came essentially from the old Scottish border auriculas which she recorded in her painting. 'Craig Dhu' and 'Craig Nordie', both illustrated, were very old varieties found in a garden in Glen Muick by Alex Duguid and named by him after two local Deeside hills. One or two of the show auriculas would grow in the garden, but her list in the 1970s carried a selection that included 'Old Lavender', in a dusky light purple, the red and yellow 'Dusty Miller', their foliage so covered in white meal

that they would appear as though they had very little leaf, 'Blue Velvet', not only scented but a clear blue with a white eye, bronze yellow and a yellow green with the addition of the 'Old Suffolk Bronze'. In my opinion one of the loveliest paintings that she ever made of an auricula was one of the pale blue grey which she called 'Mrs. Cairns' Blue' (see Plate 40). There is a softness to the colour and the gentle outline of the flower that is almost breathtaking in its beauty.

The name *auricula ursi* literally means 'bear's ear'. This is what the leaf is supposed to resemble. The Reverend C. Oscar Moreton

Plate 66. Auricula 'Craig Nordie'.

preferred the classical legend from *The Retir'd Gardener* by London & Wise, 1706. It was a translation from the French and the story ran like this. Auricula was originally called Anthilla, a daughter of the garden of the Hesperides; her mother was the shepherdess Icmasia. She was the favourite child and great care was taken of her. Greatly admired for her beauty, she had many lovers and was a skilled needlewoman who spent many hours contemplating the gods and especially the constellation of the She Bear,

to whom she would frequently offer vows and for whom she would burn aromatic herbs. One hot day she went to celebrate the feast of Priapus, in a nearby village, but, not being used to the heat, she suffered a brain seizure, and died a few days later. Cliperus and Icmasia were not to be comforted and the She Bear, in return for her devotion, changed her into a flower which she called auricula.

The auriculas which Mary grew were not, like Anthilla, of a weakly constitution. They are

Plate 67. Auricula, 'Old Wine'.

Plate 68. Auricula, 'Suffolk Bronze'.

Plate 69. Auricula 'Old Aberdeenshire Yellow'.

Plate 70. Auricula 'Gordon Harrison'.

easily propagated by taking off the small offsets in late spring and by potting them on they will produce a single flowering stem the following year. They can also be easily grown from seed, but only the strongest ever flower in the first year. Rather like the double primrose, the Barnhaven strain will produce a good selection of double flowers, but for some reason they did not appeal to Mary with her roots deep into the flowers she had known and her love of the Scots gardens of her childhood. I am frequently surprised by the longevity of some of the cultivars which, like Mary who did not die until she was one hundred and one, seem to go on for ever.

CHAPTER 6
Daisies

Plate 71. Hen and Chickens daisy.

The daisy, like the primrose, can make an honest claim to have been the first English garden plant. A ploughman walking home, seeing one which is slightly different and planting it by his back door, is not planting it there for food or medicinal purposes. Mary was well aware of this; she, like me, was charmed once more with Margery Fish writing in *Cottage Garden Flowers* in 1961:

No self respecting garden would be without its little edging of daisies. Rather prim and always well behaved nothing could fit in better with the narrow paths and edgings of shells or bricks. Daisies prefer a moist situation so grow well beneath the dripping eaves and make gay little borders at the bottom of the cottage walls or peeping through the fence against the road.

Plate 72. Hen and Chickens daisy.

Plate 73. Hen and Chickens daisy.

Mary liked the history of the daisy, which was used in early medicine. Dioscorides discussed uses for daisy-like types of chrysanthemum style flowers, while Pliny wrote of a white flower inclining to red that grew in the fields which, if applied with *Artemisia,* was very efficacious for troubles of the eye. The daisy had an 'eye' which was used in early English medicine to treat eye conditions. The Anglo-Saxons became quite enthusiastic and would pour ale and holy water over daisies and sing a charm designed to ensure that the baneful sores of water elf disease 'neither burn nor burst, nor find their way further, nor turn foul and fallow,

nor thump and throb on, nor be wicked wounds nor dig deeply down'. This was then able to cure a man who had livid nails, watering eyes and who looked continually downwards.

The Welsh use of the daisy was much more prosaic. An important part of Welsh national history, it commenced with Rhiwallon, the house physician to Rhys ap Gruffyd (Rhys the Hoarse), Lord of Dinevor, who died in 1233. He was the son of a poor cowherd and the fabulously beautiful Lady of the Lake, Llyn-y-VanVach. She would make mysterious entrances into his life, then return to the lake, her home. Eventually she abandoned the lake

Plate 74. Parkinson's Great White double daisy.

and settled down with the cowherd, making him extremely rich. Her father said she must return home if her husband struck her without anger three times. One knock with a pair of gloves and two other simple accidental blows meant that she had to return home to the lake, leaving her three sons. All three sons knew of their mother's origins and would wander along the lakeside, hoping that they would see her. One day she appeared to Rhiwallon, the eldest, and told him that he would help all mankind by relieving pain and curing sickness. She pointed out various herbs, among which was the daisy. Rhiwallon then received his earliest training. His success was so famous that Rhys ap Gruffyd gave him the estate called Myddvai. It was little use to him in his lifetime as he had to stay in the castle, treat everyone for nothing

and ride with his master to battle. His proverbs ring across the centuries:

He who goes to bed supperless will have no need of Rhiwallon of Myddvai
A light dinner, less supper, sound sleep, a long life
Drink water like an ox; and wine like a king.
GOD WILL SEND FOOD TO WASHED HANDS.

It was unusual in the Middle Ages to have such emphasis placed on cleanliness and this may have helped the family's long line of success. The last descendant of the Lady of the Lake died on 12 May 1842 at the then venerable age of eighty-five. He left behind two manuscripts

Plate 75. 1. *Ranunculus aconitifolius* Fair Maids of France (Kent). 2. *Aquilegia* Granny's Bonnet, double. 3. *Bellis perennis* 'Alice', double daisy. 4. *Bellis perennis* 'Prolifera', Hen and Chickens daisy. 5. *Bellis perennis* 'Dresden China', double daisy, pink. 6. *Bellis perennis* 'Robert', double daisy, white.

From: Mrs. MARGERY FISH.

EAST LAMBROOK MANOR,
SOUTH PETHERTON, SOM.

Tel.: South Petherton 328.

Dear Mrs. McMurtrie,   Mar 10 1959.

Thank you very much for your letter.
I am very pleased to hear from you because I
always remember with great pleasure my visit
to you or your garden.

I am enclosing my lists so if you
want to exchange at any time I shall be
delighted. I expect I am too late to add to
my order. I seem to have lost my white Dresden
China daisy again so would like a plant
of Robert from you one time. The pink one
does wonderfully for me but I can't keep the
white.

I can sympathise with you. My garden is
full of weeds and the soil so waterlogged that
I can't do much about it. It is a lovely time of
year but I wish there were more hours in
the day —
        All good wishes
            Yours sincerely.
                Margery Fish

Plate 76. Letter from Margery Fish to Mary McMurtrie.

for study: the flowers of the native hills predominate, but the daisy could remove warts, cure insanity, malignant smallpox and clear the eyes. Its final use was to tell if a patient would live or die. 'Take the flower of a daisy pound it well with wine and offer as a drink. If he vomits he will die, he will live if he can keep it down. And this has been proven.' Anyone who has tasted the bitterness of the daisy flower and knows how unpleasant it can be could possibly reverse the interpretation.

John Parkinson records in his *Paradisus* of 1629 an illustration of the double flowering Hen and Chickens daisy, one flower producing many smaller surrounding ones (Plates 71 to 73). It remains among the easiest of the old daisies to grow although I lost mine to the dreaded daisy rust. Mary's daughter Jean was able to send me some more, but they too

Plate 77. *Bellis perennis* 'Dresden China' daisy.

Plate 78. *Bellis perennis* 'Alice'.

Plate 79. *Bellis perennis* 'Rob Roy'.

succumbed to the Australian daisy rust like all the rest except Parkinson's old double white (Parkinson's 'Great White' – see Plate 74) which seems to have the strength to throw off the disease. Mary sent some Hen and Chickens daisies to Margery Fish who was fascinated by them. She found splitting them a great panacea in times of stress, a fact which quite coincidentally Mary did as well.

The daisy has three principal colours white, pink, and crimson. It is sub-divided by the size and shape of the flowers. During the 1870s the Hen and Chickens daisy was reputed to be available in crimson, but I have never seen a plant or known a reliable source. There is a dwarf double daisy which goes under the name of 'Robert' (Plates 75 and 76) in the South of England and 'The Pearl' in the North; small and compact, it is rather slow growing compared with the more commonly occurring form called 'Alba Plena'. I would like to say that I could never distinguish this from the form called 'Miss Mason' and am inclined to think that they are the same plant.

The pink forms of the daisy are more distinct. The smaller of the two called 'Dresden China' (Plates 75 to 77) is strong growing and, if well established, will flower through the winter. The larger and far more fugitive cultivar is called 'Alice' (Plate 78). This is interesting because the crimson form of this, 'Rob Roy' (Plates 79 and 80), is reputed to have an association with Sir Walter Scott. It was widely used at Belvoir Castle at the turn of the nineteenth century when W.H. Divers, Head Gardener to the Duke of Rutland, was creating the famous Spring Gardens there. When he took over the Blackbutts Nursery, David Chalmers, the son of William Chalmers, nurseryman of Stonehaven, Kincardineshire, once found that his plants of 'Alice' sported crimson. He was able to propagate this, at one time selling it as 'Red Alice'. It was, however, indistinguishable from 'Rob Roy', so this may well have been its source. I have always found that this is the most susceptible of all plants to the daisy rust and although biosysthane gives a reasonable protection if it has to be sprayed four times in a season the spray will damage the root system.

Margery Fish had a small crimson daisy which was sent to her from Ireland. Never more than two inches (five centimetres) high, it was a plant which gave her much pleasure for its neat, trim habit. It was fugitive. In the early

1990s I returned some thirty plants to East Lambrook Manor, but I presume they, like mine, have now fallen victim to the Australian daisy rust. Howard Rice, the photographer, did make a slide of it in its final flowering so that it is recorded. A similar fate almost applies to another that Mary enjoyed. Grown commercially by David Chalmers and called the Staffordshire daisy, it was similar in colour to Hen and Chickens but without chicks. Recently I sent Angela Winfield of Snape Cottage some plants of 'Miss Mason' and the single Hen and Chickens. She sent me a small weak side shoot of the Staffordshire. I potted it in a good compost, gave it an aspirin and it has now thrown a new leaf. Aspirin is a valuable tonic for all sickly plants. Mary thought that the crimson and white form of daisy that at one time Abriachan Nurseries, Inverneside, sold was the form known as 'Bon Accord' which was being grown in nurseries in Scotland well into the 1950s.

I once sent David Chalmers a very tough little single blue daisy called *Bellis rotundifolia* 'Caerulescens'. It had single flowers of a delightful mid blue. Despite the fact that it is loved by slugs, it has the best resistance of all daisies to the dreaded rust. He found it a good seller. Monksilver Nurseries sell a form of single daisy called 'Dawn Raider' which has a good variegation on its leaves. The flowers, however, are not exceptional and, rather like the green ugly daisy called 'Oddbod', it is more curious than beautiful.

When the Australian daisy rust arrived in England in the early 1990s it was first seen along the South Coast, gradually working northwards. Consequently it was here in Cambridgeshire some years before it moved to Scotland and it does not seem to have made the inroads on the old daisies in Scotland that it has done with us in the South. My letters to Mary obviously made her alarmed enough to record as many as possible. I believe she always regretted never having recorded the breathtaking beauty of the old double primroses sufficiently before they went. Indeed, fifty years on I remember the glowing crimson of 'Madame de Pompadour', the soft grey blue of 'Prince Silverwings' and the clear picotee edges of 'Bon Accord Beauty' and 'Bon Accord Elegans'.

Modern daisies in garden centres have their season of growth, flower and die. For Mary, and indeed for all her friends and correspondents, their size and clumsiness did not capture the romance of the past centuries that the old daisies had. In my opinion the Australian daisy rust is losing its original vigour and, since these daisies have no way of creating a genetic resistance, it is to be hoped that they may slowly regain their original strength.

CHAPTER 7
Pinks and Carnations

But what shall I say of the Queene of delight and of flowers, Carnations and Gilloflowers, whose bravery, variety and sweete smell joined together, tyeeth everyone's affection with greate earnestness, both to like and to have them

wrote Parkinson in 1629. Mary did not grow carnations in the quantity and variety that she did pinks. She found pinks more historically rewarding. We had some correspondence around 1999 when I sent her one or two blooms to paint (see Plate 31). One was of 'Afton Water', a carnation which when I was a child an uncle of mine grew; the other was of Margery Fish's double dark red, which Margery considered to be the oldest carnation she grew. Pliny, writing in the first century A.D., states that they were discovered in Spain in the days of Caesar Augustus. The Spaniards used it to give a spicy flavour to all beverages. The story of Colonel Fenbow and the 'Fenbow Nutmeg Clove' which had been grown in the Lake District since the seventeenth century to flavour wine was one with which we were all well acquainted.

The pink was a native of Eastern Europe, later introduced to gardens. Mary was interested in John Tradescant's voyage to Russia in 1618. 'One of the Emporer's boats to carri him from Iland to Iland to see what thinges grewe upon them' finding 'Pinkes growing naturall of the beste sorte we have here in Ingland, with the eges of the leaves deeply cut or jaged very finely'. The reason for her interest was travel. Parkinson wrote of his plants for the joy of growing them as a gardener, but Tradescant rarely with the joy of growing,

almost more of a collector. There was a time I put a great deal of research into this with no effect. All I found was that there was seemingly epilepsy in the Tradescant family (skulls in family portraits often meant this) but there remains no specific reason why Parkinson had become the inspiration for the conservation of old plants.

The earlier pinks of the sixteenth and seventeenth century were mostly single and were not as highly prized as the carnation. The Reverend Oscar Moreton always said that if carnations were gold then pinks would be silver. This was not really such a damning fact. In 1676 John Rea wrote:

Pinks are of many sorts and of little esteem, they only serve to set the sides of borders in spacious gardens, and some of them for posies, mixed with the beds of Damask Roses Most of them are single and there are some double flowers, the best, those that are called 'feathered pinkies'.

It was not until the eighteenth century that the laced pink or Paisley pink appeared.

Mary had a particular affection for pinks because they had introduced her to George Morrison Taylor. Long before our correspondence had commenced I had read his book on *Old Fashioned Flowers* and greatly enjoyed his scholarship. The destruction of his papers by his executors stopped the publication of the book on old pinks which Mary was illustrating, but he had introduced her to the possibilities of recreating some of the old florists' pinks. Her paintings of these, later published in her book *Old Cottage Pinks*,

Plate 80. The Fenbow Nutmeg Clove Carnation.

Plate 81. Old Border carnation.

represent the record we have of an attempt to recreate some of the old florists' pinks.

As true Scots they both wished to see continuation of the culture of the Paisley pink; they were deeply interested in its history. I wrote the details of them out for Mary towards the end of her life and encountered an interesting fact. The shows of pinks which the Paisley weavers held to give them ideas for the patterns of Paisley shawls took place between June and October. My conclusion was that *Dianthus plumarius* is a native of Eastern Europe, which was crossed with some seeds of *Dianthus sinensis*. This unscented biennial dianthus was widely used in illustrations of porcelain and pottery from Persia to Japan. I concluded this because the ordinary *Dianthus plumarius* only flowers in June, but *sinensis,* although a shortlived perennial, flowers from June until the frosts. Rory McEwen, a fellow Scot and a great illustrator of flowers, painted 'William Brownhill', 'Murray's Laced Pink' and 'Paisley Gem', but only 'Paisley Gem' could be certainly considered from the period. It was raised by a muslin worker called John Macree who died in 1804. He was so delighted in having grown this new seedling of almost perfect florists' standards that he gave a plant to King George III who had an interest in these flowers.

Mary liked to differentiate the varieties by their age. In her opinion the oldest pinks she grew were probably the old fringed white and pink. These she considered were those which were probably referred to in John Rea's *Flora, Ceres and Pomona*. She enjoyed these pinks for their calm sweet scent. However, they were challenged by the 'Painted Lady' of Parkinson for age. He refers to a Mr. Bradshaw 'His Dainty Lady' whose colouring could well have helped to become the forerunner of the laced pink. In the opinion of many growers this name changed over the century into 'Painted Lady'. Both single and double forms, however, remain good garden plants today.

In 1965 Mary revised her plant list, heading it Primroses, Pinks and Alpines. This revealed more than one would have thought of her

Plate 82. Old Border carnation. 20 August 1973.

Plate 83. Carnation 'Admiral Lord Anson'. Mrs. Hughes.

preference for plants. She always had difficulty keeping the old pinks going once she moved to Balbithan. In my opinion the reason for this was that nearer the coast at Aberdeen the sea winds carried sufficient salt to keep the thrips at bay. In Balbithan garden there was more shelter and thrips sucking the very life blood of the plant made their propagation more difficult. This did not deter her work, however, in growing and painting what she considered a lasting part of our gardening heritage. The 'Brympton Red' pink which Lady Lilian Digby found at the workhouse in Beaminster was a great favourite. Margery Fish had distributed it widely, it was a

Plate 84. Unnamed Flake carnation.

Plate 85. Border carnations from Mr. Argo, Aberdeen. 1973.

good grower and as a painter Mary enjoyed the brilliant velvety crimson. However, it did not challenge the 'Cockenzie Pink' in her eyes; some locally called it the 'Montrose Pink'. She dated it to 1720 and it fulfilled for her all she wanted in a garden plant. Fully fringed with a double rosy centre and a sound Scots ancestry, this became one of her very loved garden plants. A similar type was the one known as 'Chelsea Pink' or 'The Little Old Lady'; once again the fringed petals represented a challenge to the painter, while the bright crimson flowers laced with white gave the memory of days gone past.

It is difficult when discussing pinks to place the popular 'Mrs. Sinkins'. Easily grown and highly scented, its only fault is that it splits its calyx and can get very battered in wet weather. It was named after the wife of the workhouse master in Slough and has found its way into the heart of the nation by representation on the coat of arms of that town. Queen Victoria would drive over from Windsor when they were in flower to enjoy the scent. Another called 'Musgrave's Pink' is reputed to have been used by the early Spanish flower painters. This has to be considered as possibly coming from Holland originally; with its single flower and a good clear green eye it represents a most interesting and easily grown cultivar.

The laced pinks were always a challenge. They are not so easily grown as the popular pinks. We have discussed 'Paisley Gem', but another old one found by the garden writer A.J. Macself in an old garden was always referred to as 'Dad's Favourite'. This had clearly marked edges and remains an easily grown cultivar. 'Paddington', grown on the site of what is now Paddington station by Thomas Hogg in the early nineteenth century, was one which she always enjoyed with its small rose pink deeply fringed petals. Somehow she could forgive a split calyx, a fact which upset many exhibitors of the flowers. She grew 'Madonna' – not named after the singer – and also 'Sam Barlow' with its large rather clumsy white flower and an almost black centre.

Although Mary's last book was *Old Cottage Pinks*, illustrating many from the garden she

Plate 86. Picotee carnation. 1973.

created at Sunhoney, as the years passed she seemed to get less pleasure from pinks than in the earlier times, possibly because there was no one hybridising them as had been the case shortly after the war. At that time F.R. McQuown and Montagu Allwood were consciously trying to recreate the old laced pinks, with great success. George Morrison Taylor found some of the old pinks, but sadly there is no record left of his hybridisation, other than Mary's paintings. These paintings stare at us today as the memory of the inspiration of the pleasure that so many have received from the Paisley shawls of the past.

Old Pinks.

Mary A. McMurtrie
1976.

Plate 88. *Dianthus deltoides.*

Plate 87. Old pinks.

Plate 89. Garden pinks growing at Balbithan House.

Plate 90. The sweet william.

CHAPTER 8
Roses

Plate 91. *Rosa mundi.*

The move to Balbithan meant Mary's immense knowledge of growing plants became more concentrated. Her interest in green gardens was extended. Her knowledge of the history of the rose meant she was principally growing plants which flowered at the most for one month; rarely did the roses she grew have the ability to flower repeatedly.

The use of roses for decoration is well recorded since Roman times and during the Middle Ages the rose was largely associated with the Virgin Mary. She grew them because

Plate 92. 1. *Rosa filipes* 'Kiftsgate'. Long pointed leaflets, flowers cup-shaped, buds pinkish. Very few thorns. 2. *Rosa longicuspis.* Leaves more rounded, glossy green, buds creamy, petals larger, more widespread, flower opens flat.

Plate 93. The Garland Rose.

they had the style and quality that suited the garden at Balbithan.

The roses fell into three separate parts. In the first case there were the old roses that could be associated with Balbithan; their antiquity suited the style of the garden and some of these were already growing there when she arrived. Second were the antiquities she found in her

Plate 94. *Rosa brunonii* 'Betty Sherriff'.

Plate 95. Wild rose seedling, four petals, from Himalayas.

Plate 96. Rose, four petals, Himalayas, very leafy.

Plate 97. *Rosa villosa,* found near Ballater by Alex Duguid.

search for the Scots rose. Third was the Scots rose itself, a rose on which she could have confidently claimed to have been the most knowledgeable amateur in Scotland.

On arrival at Balbithan Mary saw the necessity of making the garden into separate compartments to contain the great number of plants that she wished to grow. It was natural that

Plate 98. Double green rose from St. Andrews, old garden. Approx. 3–4ft bush.

low hedging should be found and, entranced with the large numbers of roses that had survived the neglect in the garden, she chose *Rosa mundi* for a wind breaking hedge. This was a most successful planting because although it only grows about six feet (two metres) high, it flowers best when rather starved. The rainfall at Balbithan meant that the soil, although inherently fertile, was never over rich.

As well as being an ideal hedging plant for the garden, this rose gave Mary much that she wished to capture on paper. Almost every petal was differently coloured, meaning that the desire to capture the shades and the light was a constant challenge. She enjoyed its historical association, being called the York and Lancaster rose by Parkinson. 'I have seen roses damasked red and white' said Shakespeare in the Sonnets; the crimson, pink and white flowers on the same bush gave it a charm in the garden that totally complemented the walls of the castle.

Among the climbing roses were a few which were great favourites of both Margery Fish and Vita Sackville-West: *Rosa filipes* 'Kiftsgate', *R. longicuspis*, and the Garland rose. What Mary always termed Betty Sherriff's rose – given to her by Mollie Harbord – was a species grown from seed sent from Bhutan. A four-petalled rose from the Himalayas was also grown from seed brought home by her son-in-law, Tony Gardner. *Rosa villosa* was found near Ballater by Alex Duguid. Others included the double

Plates 99 and 100. *Rosa farreri* var. *persetosa*.

green rose from China introduced in the early nineteenth century, and *Rosa farreri* var. *persetosa*, the threepenny-bit rose and *Rosa dupontii*.

The next group were roses which were delightful in their own right. Roses like 'Gloire de Dijon', which few can fault, 'Champney's Pink Cluster', 'New Dawn' and 'Fantin-Latour', 'Variegata di Bologna' (because the almost black and white markings were never repeated twice on the same rose petal) and 'Madame Alfred Carrière'. One thing they had in common was an all-pervading scent. When the roses were blooming on a still day the garden would have thrilled Eleanour Sinclair Rohde who had this dream from the Renaissance that on walking into a garden you needed to have every sensation a man can experience.

Finally came roses like *Rosa* x *alba* 'Alba

Maxima', the Jacobite rose, *Rosa* x *alba* 'Alba Semiplena', the hybrid of *Rosa moyesii*, the Learney Rose, also known as 'Wolley Dodd', the dog rose, small but very clear, delightful for detailed painting, and the almost black gallica called 'Tuscany Old Velvet'. She mixed this with a white climbing rose originally in the garden at Balbithan when she arrived.

Most important, however, were Mary's moss roses. The moss at the base of the calyx comes from the glands which are always present in cabbage and alba roses. The moss rose, as we know it, first appeared in the early eighteenth century at the Botanic Garden in Leiden; it was claimed by the French M. Faguet in 1845 who stated that it had been known in 1696 in Carcasonne, but Frerard Du Castel, whose book is reputed to contain the reference, does not do this according to Edward Bunyard in his *Old Garden Roses*. For want of a more conclusive

Plate 101. *Rosa dupontii.*

Plate 102. *Rosa* 'Gloire de Dijon'. 1984.

Plate 103. *Rosa* 'Champney's Pink Cluster'. November 1981.

Plate 104. *Rosa* 'Champney's Pink Cluster'. 1985.

Plate 105. *Rosa* 'Fantin-Latour'.

Plate 106. Above. Bourbon rose 'Variegata di Bologna'. Below. Unnamed.

Plate 107. *Rosa* x *alba* 'Alba Maxima'.

Plate 108. *Rosa* x *alba* 'Alba Semiplena' ('Jacobite rose').

Plate 109. Climbing rose originally in the garden at Balbithan.

Plate 110. Moss rose from Strathdon.

Plate 111. Monymusk rose, *Rosa cinnamomea plena*. July 2000.

Plate 112. *Rosa cinnamomea plena*, 'Rose de Mai', June 1974. Mary called this the Monymusk rose and had the name verified by Graham Thomas. It grows by the side of the path leading from Monymusk village to Paradise Woods. Flowers <u>very</u> double, packed with tightly folded petals. Leaves smooth, grey-green on back, with reddish mid-ribs. Five leaflets. Stems smooth, chestnut-brown and shiny with thorns set only in pairs, at junction of stems.

claim it must remain with the Dutch. Mary had a friend who lived in Strathdon in whose garden grew an old pink moss rose; it always remained one of her favourite roses and she painted it time and again.

The Monymusk rose was not a musk rose.

It was, in my opinion, a rose that made the transition from the wild to the garden, to the all-important Scots rose on which Mary wrote a most decorative and knowledgeable book.

Mary's interest in the Scots rose grew with the delight she gained from visiting the gardens

Plate 113. Burnet Rose, *Rosa spinosissima*. June.

that still contained some of the old bushes. Interest in them was declining. For example, in 1933 when Edward Bunyard wrote his book on *Old Garden Roses* he was able to list over thirty cultivars. By the 1970s it was hard for Mary to find this number and variety of colour. The search continued because it centred around the most important features of her life. She was gently proud of her Scots ancestry and she enjoyed the ancient memories that some of these roses carried. The plants themselves fitted into the character of the garden she was creating at Balbithan. More importantly, these roses did not flaunt themselves; they maintained the modesty which she had tried to maintain in her life and her garden.

The Scots rose grows on the sandy dunes and river banks, usually on the poorest soil in a low tangle of prickly bushes. It is characterised by thorny stems, five petalled solitary white

flowers on short leafy sprigs set alternately along the branches. Mary enjoyed its tiny leaflets, its fresh clear scent, but most importantly the round dark hips of varying colours and form which appeared in the autumn. It is, of course, the hardiest of roses, growing from Iceland to Siberia, Turkey and Central Asia. In Europe it grows as far south as Armeria in Spain, it is used as a hedge in Russia, and even maintains a foothold on the windswept limestone cliffs of The Burren in Southern Ireland.

Originally called the Pimpinell rose or *Rosa pimpinellifolia* and now called *Rosa spinosissima*, it is also known as the Burnet rose. One of its earliest descriptions is by Dodoens in the translation of his *Herbal* of 1575:

Amongst the kindes of wilde roses, there is founde a sorte whose shutes, twigges and

Plate 114. Scots roses. 1. Double white. 2. Double cream. 3. 'Williams' Double Yellow'. 4. Single cream.

branches are covered all over with thicke small thornie prickles. The flowers be small single and white, and of a good savour. The whole plante is base and lowe, and the leaste of al both the garden and wilde kinde of roses.

Gerard records in his *Herball* of 1597:

The Pimpinell rose is likewise one of the wilde ones whose stalkes shoot forth from the ground in many places the height of one or two cubits, of a browne coloure and armed with sharp prickles, which divide themselves towards the tips into divers branches, whereupon growe leaves consisting of divers small ones, set upon a middle rib, like those of burnet, which is called in latin pimpinella, whereupon it was called *Rosa pimpinella* the Burnet Rose.

The first mention that Mary was able to find of the Burnet rose being called the Scots rose was in a bill dated 1775 for plants supplied to the Countess of Oxford by John and William Perfect of Pontefract:

4 Burnet leaved roses 1s.4d.
2 Red Scotch roses 2s.
2 white Scotch roses 1s.4d.

In 1793 Robert Brown and his brother transplanted some of the wild roses from the Hill of Kinnoul near Perth into their nursery garden. One had flowers slightly tinged red from which a plant was raised as if one or two flowers had come from one bud. It produced seed from whence came some semi-double flowers. By continuing the raising of more plants from seed between 1802 and 1803 they had eight good varieties. They subsequently increased the number and from the stock in the Perth garden the nurseries of both Scotland and England were supplied. From this small beginning the Scots rose became very popular. Robert Austin of Glasgow bred them and by 1820 there were many collections created. In 1830 the *Hortus Britannicus* gave 177 varieties of which 147 had

names. The unnamed ones gave colours like double crimson and light marbled. Sadly only four of the named cultivars in the *Hortus Britannicus* are still grown today. These are 'Fulgens', 'Falkland', 'Loch Leven' and 'Staffa'. Mary was always surprised that all this had come out of the wild rose from the Hill of Kinnoul.

The Scots roses were welcome as spring merged into summer. They had come to popularity at the moment when there was increasing interest in gardening generally, and wild gardening in particular. For example, Gertrude Jekyll in *Roses for English Gardens* wrote:

The Scotch Briers are excellent plants for many kinds of use, but are perhaps best of all in wild banks with Heaths and Cistuses…These fine hardy Briers have also one merit that most Roses lack, for in winter the leafless crowd of close-growing plentifully-prickled branches forms masses of warm bronze colouring that have quite a comforting appearance. The pretty Briers might well replace the dull and generally ugly steep slopes of turf that disfigure so many gardens… they are equally in place in the humblest garden and the most exalted… and for all sorts of uses they hardly ever come amiss.

She grew them round her house at Munstead Wood.

E.A. Bowles wrote in *My Garden in Summer*, still one of the greatest garden trilogies ever written:

I have a great affection for most of them, from the dwarf native form, with its small cream coloured flowers, to the double garden raised forms known as Scotch Briers… I could almost believe that *Rosa spinosissima* represents the first attempts of the Gods in fashioning the rose, for its dwarf wild form is a centre from which branch off so many different types.

Despite the fact that they have but one short period of flower and despite the fact that there

Plate 115. *Rosa* 'Céline Forestier'.

were increasing quantities of repeat flowering roses on the market, the Scots rose continued to find a place, however diminished, in the garden. Mary wrote in her book *Scots Roses*:

> They have great charm and one has only to see a bush or a hedge in the full flush of flowering on a sunny June day, and enjoy the scent which spreads all over the garden, to realise how delightful they are and how much we would miss them.

The rose hips are among the most attractive of all berries throughout the winter.

The Scots rose appears in Scots history at the time of Bonnie Prince Charlie. The story of Prince Charlie's rose recounted to her by her friend Alex Duguid from the records of Edrom Nursery where he worked with the Misses Logan-Home was the very essence of what Mary tried to preserve in our gardening heritage.

On the evening after the battle of Prestonpans in 1745, where Charles Stuart defeated the Government troops commanded by Johnnie Cope, a reception was held in the ballroom of Holyrood Palace. The Prince wore on his coat a double white rose. The morning after the Prince had gone the chambermaid found the rose left on the dressing table in the bedroom. She took it home to her mother, a keen gardener, who managed to root the rose spray. Eventually the resulting plant was planted in the gardens of Carberry Towers, where it flourished. Many years later Mrs. Cowan, the eldest sister of Miss Mollie Logan-Home of Edrom, was taking tea with Lady Elphinstone, who gave her plants of this rose. Mrs. Cowan in turn gave plants to her sister who planted them in the gardens of Edrom House, Duns, Berwickshire. In 1925 when the Misses Logan-Home moved the Nursery to Silverwells, near Coldingham, the rose was planted there. It soon developed into a large bush, increasing itself by suckers. Mary treasured this plant above all the other Scots roses, feeling it a living link to the Scotland she felt was changing for ever.

In the garden of her early childhood there had been a large old bush Scots rose; she never forgot the scent of the double yellow flowers. When she saw the garden at Balbithan she found five different ones which had been there since 1840 when she estimated the garden had been last restored – two pink, a marbled rose pink, a semi-double deep rose, and a lovely two coloured one which she believed from the description to be 'Mary Queen of Scots'. It was not in her nature to stop collecting the various cultivars once she had seized upon a species to decorate the garden. She added others as she found them in the area, sometimes even by ruined cottages. Two pink, a white and a yellow from the Manse garden of Echt were used to create a hedge. Later two were found at Craigevar Castle and from Crathes Castle she brought 'William III'. She recorded all the cultivars that she had found in her book on Scots roses.

Gordon Rowley, in his article 'The Scotch Rose and its Garden Descendants' (RHS *Journal*, October 1961), states that the wild populations of *Rosa spinosissima* vary extensively in habit, armature, leaf serration, indumentum and flower colour. It is probable that from this wide variation Prince Charlie's rose occurred. It concerned Mary greatly that she could never find the garden where this rose originated. The other Jacobite roses engraved on glasses to toast the King over the Water, *Rosa x alba* 'Alba Maxima' and *Rosa x alba* 'Semiplena', are always at the centre of any discussion on Scots roses as to which is the true Scots rose. No one has ever decided, certainly, which is the true rose. Mary would have liked the one chosen by the Prince after Prestonpans to have been correct.

Nowadays it is increasingly difficult to find representative selections of these roses. In 1974 Dr. and Mrs. Peter Waister and Mrs. Dorothy Park laid out a small rose garden in the village of Kinnaird near Inchture in Perthshire. Scots roses dominate the plantings. In the opinion of Mary this was most appropriate, for it was here, close to the Hill of Kinnoul in the Carse of Gowrie, that the double Scots roses were first raised in Robert Brown's nursery.

Plate 116. *Rosa moschata* 'Semiplena', the autumn-flowering musk rose.

CHAPTER 9
Forgotten Elizabethan Plants

There were a group of plants which Mary considered essential to the atmosphere she wished to create at Balbithan to give the garden the gentle feeling of times past but not forgotten. The first of these was the wallflower. At first sight not an important plant, it had two cultivars she greatly treasured. The first of these was the double yellow now in commerce as 'Harpur Crewe' (see page 55) and the second was the double red splashed with yellow better known as 'Old Bloody Warrior'.

The wallflower has a long history in our gardens and for the Scots has possibly an even grander association than the thistle. Elizabeth, daughter of the Earl of March, was betrothed to the heir of the King of Scotland, Robert III. She had fallen in love with the son of a border chieftain, Scott of Tushielaw. He disguised himself as a minstrel and came and sang beneath her window, suggesting in his song a means of eloping. She dropped a sprig of wallflower at his feet to show that she understood his song, but in her excitement she did not fasten the rope securely and fell to her death. Scott then became a travelling minstrel wearing a sprig of wallflower in his hat. This became widely copied and added to the fame of the legend

Known in mediaeval literature as Cheiry, Cheirisaunce and Chevisaunce, and even the Stock Gilloflower, eventually the wall gilloflower became the wallflower and the stock gilloflower became the stock, the yellow one being the wallflower. This plant will survive on a wall but, indeed, will grow vastly better in a good lime rich well-drained alkaline soil.

Even some of the seedling strains like 'Vulcan' in dark crimson and 'Primrose Dame'

are gathering the years, having been used for spring bedding for the past hundred years or so. For the Scots the variety called 'Harpur Crewe' in double dwarf yellow has a history far more ancient than the 'Reverend Henry Harpur Crewe' under which name it lives in commerce. Its origin is from the fortress where Marmion and Douglas had their encounter. Here it was discovered again by a lady whose ancestry came from Tantallon Castle. She gave her plants of this to George Morrison Taylor who recorded the incident in his *Book of Old Fashioned Flowers* in 1946. Mary and he were saddened that plants that were essentially Scots in their associations were not used more widely, particularly when this plant is as easy as a *Pelargonium* to propagate. After flowering fresh shoots will appear and, if they are taken with about six leaves, cut level, and kept in damp sand, they will easily propagate. Even the small side shoots will provide plants that flower in the second year.

The second of the wallflowers that Mary considered to be important was the one called 'Old Bloody Warrior' (and called 'Bloody Old Warrior' by Margery Fish when she was propagating it). It is probably the double red wallflower which Parkinson records in his *Paradisus* in 1629. It does not have the vigour of 'Harpur Crewe' and does not have a strong constitution, but it is not impossible to grow. In the days before meristem propagation made all things possible, I had already realised that if you took the growing point of a cutting, rooted it and repeated this three times then the plant would grow with renewed vigour. I now find that it grows much more easily than it did when I first began gardening. Frequently in the

Plate 117. Wallflower – wild.

Plate 118. The Stock Gilliflower.

Plate 119. Dames Violet, Sweet Rocket.

Plate 120. Old Rose Plantain.

period 1950 to 1975 writers called it extinct or impossible to grow, but that is no longer the case.

The double flowering sweet rocket *Hesperis matronalis* 'Flore Pleno' has always been a very prized plant. The single form is easily grown and will survive in the wild garden; not so the double which seems to concentrate on its scent (see Plate 34). In 1597 Gerard wrote of it in its single state as Dames Violets or Queene Gilliflowers. In *The Garden of Pleasant Flowers* (1629) Parkinson calls it *Hesperis pannonica* or the Dames Violet of Hungary; later in his *Theatrum Botanicum* he says that he has received the true double flowering form from Dr. Anthony Sadler, physician of Exeter. As always, with these early books, contradictions arise, but *The Garden Book of Sir Thomas Hanmer* (1659, first published in 1933) states:

Hesperis Rockett or the Queenes Gilloflower, beareth a stalke full of very sweet dowble white flowers in May and requires good earth and to stand in a warme place all wynter...

It had the reputation of being greatly loved in

Plate 121. 1. *Stachys lanata* − Lammies' Lugs. 2. *Endymion non-scriptus* − wild hyacinth. 3. *Centaurea montana* − mountain knapweed. 4. *Hesperis matronalis* − Rocket − Dames Violet. 5. *Lunaria* − Honesty, flower and seed. 6. *Iberis sempervirens* − Candytuft (evergreen).

France, having been a favourite flower of Marie Antoinette, particularly the white variety. During her imprisonment in the Conciergerie, Madame Richard, the concierge, was herself imprisoned for bringing her bunches of pinks, sweet rockets and tuberoses to take away the smell of the prison.

This plant was widely used for household decoration during the eighteenth and nineteenth centuries, later losing its popularity to the wider colour range of the Brompton stock. There are many suggested forms of propagation of the double sweet rocket from stripping the old flower stems to parting the roots after flowering. There is one I have always found reliable. During early March take a side slip from a larger plant as it is just coming into growth and place it in open compost in a cold frame, preferably with scant heat; the difficulty then is how not to make it root. Margery Fish had trouble rooting this plant and I remember a correspondence we had where I told her I had discovered this by using this form of propagation on *Campanula persicifolia* 'Boule de Neige', the first plant that I ever contributed to Mary's garden. The double sweet rocket was apparently extinct elsewhere by 1980 when one of the last two plants in my garden was taken for meristem propagation. As mentioned previously, I had always thought that mine had come from Margery Fish but when I was writing my book on her gardening I found a letter from me offering it to her. I am unable to come up with a source for my plant which is now available in garden centres throughout the country. To ensure that this biennial becomes perennial, always remove the flower spikes after flowering. George Morrison Taylor recorded that the Scots had a dwarf form; this is now being sold by Cally Gardens at Gatehouse of Fleet and Michael Wickenden says that it appeared as a chance variant in a group of meristem cultivars he bought for growing.

The great rose plantain *Plantago rosea* of Parkinson 1629, an Elizabethan plant, interested all three ladies, Mary, Margery and Gladys, who were sincerely attempting to save historic plants. In my opinion it was first rediscovered by Gladys Emmerson, who listed it in her nursery catalogue and it was taken up very seriously by Margery Fish. Not only did it have all the historical associations that they liked, it was a very practical green flower, particularly as Margery Fish created her green garden. It is the ordinary green plantain of the lawns and fields which Parkinson describes as:

> Instead of the long slender spike or eare that the ordinary [plantain] hath … a number of such small greene leaves lay'd round wise like unto a rose, and sometimes both these may be seene upon one and the same roote at one and the same time, which abide a great while fresh upon the roote.

I remember receiving my rose plantain from Mrs. Emmerson with a letter saying that they never came completely true from seed. It is my opinion that when this plant is in the early form of its flowering it very much resembles a double flowering green primrose. Its ease of growth gives the impression that this may well have been the reason why the double flowering green primrose was considered so easily grown in Parkinson, but the double green primrose today is one of the most difficult of all plants to grow.

The common honesty *Lunaria biennis* is widely grown. It is a useful plant to provide flower arrangers with attractive seed pods. Balbithan had a number of variants which were both interesting and attractive. The first of these was in a clear white, which of course in the long evenings was a source of great pleasure. The light hit the petals horizontally, and contrasted well with the larger flowers of the deep purple. The cultivar which gave the greatest pleasure, however, was one which was fully variegated white and purple in its petals. Tony Venison, the Gardening Editor of *Country Life,* visited my garden and remarked that in his opinion this was the most interesting plant I had flowering in May.

Forget-me-nots (*Myosotis*) are so easily grown that they are easily ignored because of their

Plate 122. Honesty.

Plate 123. The marigold.

self-seeding habit. In pink, white and blue, in varying heights and shades, they are readily available. One cultivar which was a great favourite was the perennial forget-me-never with its soft gentle blue and easy self-seeding habit; this was in complete contrast to the white form of the ordinary bedding forget-me-not whose seed is always erratic in germination. This plant originally came from the garden of E.A. Bowles at Myddelton House, Enfield. The wisest way to use this white forget-me-not is to cut off the seed heads after flowering and split it to create small bedding plants by the autumn.

Plate 124. *Cardamine pratensis,* double (Lady's smock, Cuckoo flower).

Campanula medium (Canterbury bells) was another biennial which gave great delight in later May. It does not like a heavy wet soil but grew at Balbithan with little trouble. This was one plant where the double flowering form was not favoured because the simple elegance of the old cup and saucer type appealed far more. A little known fact is that the name Canterbury bells was given to *Campanula trachelium* and what we call Canterbury bells were actually called Coventry bells. The reason that *trachelium* had the credit is because its flowers resembled the shape of the small bells with which the pilgrims adorned their horses.

Marigolds (*Calendula*) grew at Balbithan and Mary painted their bright orange discs. She preferred the old pot marigold from the cottage gardens. Less well known was the Hen and Chickens marigold which has been in our gardens for the past four hundred years. Similar in fashion to the Hen and Chickens daisy, it never reached much garden popularity because it had the habit of the chicks appearing after the main flower had died. I have grown this for many years, weeding out the not hen and chicken forms. They still look rather spiky and more curious than beautiful. The plant gets its name from the Latin *calend,* meaning that every month of the year it usually has a flower.

Cardamine pratensis, the cuckoo flower, is a flower of great beauty and, in my dry soil, difficult to grow. The double flowering form I usually grow in a pot. A relative of the bittercress, it is easy to confuse when weeding, due to the similarity of the leaf. However, the soft pale lilac of the flowers makes it a welcome addition to the garden in May. Parkinson recorded in 1629 that the double flowering form was found:

The first with a double flower is found in divers places of our owne countrey, as neer Micham about eight miles from London; also in Lancashire from where I received a plant, which perished, but was found by the industrie of a worthy gentlewoman, dwelling in those partes heretofore remembered, called Mistresse Thomasin Tunstall, a great lover of these delights. The other was sent to me by my especial good friend John Tradescant who brought it among other dainty plants from beyond the Seas, and imparted thereof a roote to me.

It is of interest that the common *Cardamine* in the Low Countries is a much darker shade than the soft lilac that we have here in the British Isles. Parkinson does not record that the plant which Tradescant gave him was a darker colour than the native. Mary got great pleasure from painting this plant because she found the twisting of the leaves arresting as they caught the light and contrasted with the pale lilac of the flowers.

At a time when Margery Fish was experimenting with ground cover and using *Pulmonaria*, Mary did not grow them in quantity, but *Pulmonaria rubra* grew at Balbithan and Sunhoney and was often painted. They had history and charm and she enjoyed the one called 'Soldiers and Sailors', whose dull crimson flowers turned blue as they aged; making it appear as though both red and blue flowers came on the same plant. Also called Joseph and Mary, its country names abound. The leaves, like an elongated heart, are marked with dull grey spots. In the tradition of herbal medicine this was widely used for treating lung disease. This attracted Mary, but the various forms did not. For example, the soft coral flowers over clear green leaves of the Christmas cowslip or Bethlehem sage, as *Pulmonaria rubra* is called, did not really

Plate 125. 1. *Vinca minor* (periwinkle) – purple, single and double blue. 2. *Pulmonaria officinalis* (lungwort) – Soldiers and Sailors, Doctrine of Signatures. 3. *Pulmonaria* – pink – Christmas Bells. 4. Sweet violets – white and blue. 5. *Primula denticulata* – Drumsticks – a later introduction, 1837, by East India Company directors.

1.

2.

3.

5.

4.

Plate 126. 1. Marsh marigolds. 2. Marsh marigolds, double form. 3. Primrose, hose-in-hose. 4. Primrose, Jack in the Green. 5. Double primrose. 6. Heartsease. 7. Double daisies. 8. Double buttercup, Fair Maids of France. 9. Double buttercup, Bachelors' Buttons. 10. Wood anemones, double.

Plate 127. *Ranunculus aconitifolius* Fair Maids of France – white. *Ranunculus acris* Bachelors' Buttons, yellow. *Ranunculus speciosus* – large greenish yellow.

Plate 128. *Viola odorata* 'Alba'.

cross her world. Nor indeed did the dark blue of a form of *Pulmonaria azurea* which the Queen Mother gave to Tony Venison as his present on leaving Sandringham having written about the garden for *Country Life* the year that King George VI died. The tough good nature of these plants and their ability to survive half shade and drought over the seasons have made them justly popular in many gardens.

The lily of the valley, *Convallaria majalis* (see page 59), was greatly enjoyed when its time of flowering arrived. Eleanour Sinclair Rohde

considered it small wonder it was the flower of Ostara, the Goddess of the Dawn in pagan times. It was its Christian symbolism, however, that attracted Mary. Its many names, like ladders to heaven where the country children would count the flower heads and say that mine has more steps than yours, or even Pentecost lilies when used for church decoration at Pentecost, all added to its attraction. For Mary as a painter it had the added attraction of the clear cream of the flower contrasting well with other plants flowering at the same time – buttercups, for

Plate 129. *Viola odorata.*

Plate 130. Dog violet. *Viola riviniana.*

example. These would then be used to contrast the colours almost as she would contrast the gold and the silver of snowdrops and aconites. Both buttercups and lily of the valley need the same conditions to flourish – a cool moist root run and the chance of getting their heads into the sun. Once established, the lily of the valley is the easier of the two as its propensity to run makes it better planted in a large container so the increasing number of cultivars do not lose their correct nomenclature.

My surprise at finishing this chapter with violets would have been far outweighed by Mary's. Gertrude Jekyll always said if you cannot grow a good bed of violets do not grow them at all. They repay good care and she advocated a new bed being propagated each year. This was one of the great flowers of British

gardening and Mary would remember the time when she was a girl when most houses would have a bunch in the room to scent the house. Now, however, there is not so much interest in them and yet they have a range of colours that give added interest if grouped together. The scent greets you before seeing the plants.

Mary liked the poetry attached to the violet, particularly the stanza written by Sir Walter Raleigh:

Sweet violets, 'Love's Paradise' that spread
Their gracious odours, which they
    couched bear
Within their paley faces

The violet always symbolised humility in the early master paintings. Botticelli is generally

Plate 131. *Viola* 'Sulfurea'. April 1990.

believed to have been the first to depict the flower with this meaning in his painting called *The Adoration,* now in the Pitti Palace in Florence. Hugo van der Goes' *Adoration of the Shepherds* has blue and white violets in the fore-ground and Eleanour Sinclair Rohde records an altarpiece in Cologne by Stephen Lochner where the Holy Child holds out His hand to His mother who in her turn carries the violet. In Eleanour's opinion the violet would not be

Plate 132. Garden violets, white and 'Coeur d'Alsace'.

such an attractive flower if it held its flower the right way up. She was not the first to notice this; Sprengel the great botanist had remarked on it two hundred years earlier, while Shakespeare used the word nodding in its traditional sense, i.e. bending downwards, in his phrase 'the nodding violet', and again:

They are as gentle
As zephyrs blowing below the violet
Not wagging his sweet head.

When John Bartram, the first great American botanist, gathered a wild violet and examined it he was so impressed with its beauty, he dreamed of it. He eventually became the founder of the first botanic garden in the New World.

The French at the time of Napoleon's exile in Elba toasted his return as Caporal Violette, or the flower that returns with the spring. Mary grew a fair range of the hardy garden cultivars. Her interest was to capture the light and the reflection of the flowers as she recorded them.

Plate 133. Violets. 'Norah Church'. 'John Raddenbury'. Giant European violet found by Mary in the Algarve. 'Coeur d'Alsace'. White violet. 'L'Arne'.

Plate 134. *Nigella damascena,* 'Love-in-a-mist' or 'Gith'.

Plate 135. The Sweet Sultan.

Grace Zambra had created new varieties in Devon in the late 1930s, but Mary preferred the older ones: 'Princess of Wales' and 'Governor Herrick' with their long stems; 'Admiral Avellan' in rich wine colour; 'Coeur d'Alsace' in delicate rose pink; 'Sulfurea', a pale apricot and the double flowering forms like the white 'Conte di Brazza' and the violet coloured 'Marie-Louise'. This was one plant where she felt a collection was well worthwhile. They

added to the garden the quality of scent in the spring which gave her pleasure.

In their cultivation she was able to avoid the mistake made by so many people in the south: violets like shade, but they also like air. Too many people plant them in good soil against a north wall and then wonder why the flowers do not grow and, even worse, why the flower stems are not long enough to pick.

Mary hoped that their popularity would

Plate 136. *Centaurea montana* – mountain knapweed – Blue Bottle Sweet Sultan.

Plate 137. *Primula denticulata* and *P. denticulata* var. *alba*.

return as people understood their growth better and they would not fail, as Byron said about Napoleon as he took leave of his adopted country:

Farewell to thee, France! But when liberty rallies
Once more in thy regions, remember me then;
The violet grows in the depth of thy valleys,
Though withered thy tears will unfold it again.

CHAPTER 10
The Final Flourish

Mary used many plants to convey interest throughout the year, some as spot plants which drew attention when they flowered and receded to the background after their growth was completed. It was not a new concept but an understanding that had grown up after the war, that as gardens became smaller they needed more individuality. This could be achieved by adding in plants of either historical or gardening interest, possibly giving an immediate flash of colour. Interest in quite a small garden could be enhanced by the discussion of the cultivation of the plant being observed.

The soil at Balbithan was helpful. Intrinsically neutral, it could have peat or lime added to accommodate a larger range of planting than many gardens. An example of this was the fact that the pinks were grown as well as a large range of gentians. Gentians are beautiful in the ethereal quality of their colour, ranging from Cambridge to Oxford blue. Although *Gentiana acaulis* grows in lime and *ascepledia* needs moist soil, they could be grown alongside *ornata, septemfida, sino-ornata* and *verna*. Carefully placed, they flowered from May to September while at the same time providing cuttings for the nursery.

Mary loved propagating. She had commenced gardening by growing alpine plants and her spirit of adventure led her to experiment with propagating some of the smaller conifers like *Chamaecyparis, Juniperus, Picea* and *Thuya*. Some of these she allowed to grow large to create structure in the garden. When they needed to be pruned she could not resist using the material to propagate for the nursery.

Sowing seed was yet another adventure and here rhododendrons were a temptation. The dwarf rhododendrons flower mainly in May and June. Other than *hirsutum* – the alpenrose – they will not tolerate lime. Mary was immensely successful in growing these dwarf rhododendrons from seed. She liked to sell them after they had flowered so she could see if there was any flower variation worth keeping. Some of these species she found more rewarding in the garden than others. Her artistic flair led her to enjoy the blue green of the leaves of *lepidostylum* followed by its primrose coloured flowers, while the flat purple crimson of *keleticum* did not appeal so greatly. The two feet (sixty centimetre) high crimson black bells of *didymum* were a good contrast to *ciliatum* which, although growing to three feet (90 centimetres), always needed protection from the morning sun. The yellow forms were a constant challenge and a delight. *Rhododendron hanceanum* 'Nanum' with creamy flowers and glossy leaves was grown for its rarity, whereas she found she could grow *sargentianum* with greater success. Generally speaking, most rhododendron colours fall between pink and purple and *R. nitens* in rosy purple grew well with *R. myrtilloides*. The range of these species was immense; at one time she had over twenty dwarf species that she sold from the nursery.

The dwarf bulbs were another challenge. Bulbs like *Allium* in its smaller species she found relatively easy to grow. *Allium moly,* the golden garlic of Gerard and Parkinson, was a good standby, but *farreri, macranthum* and *cernuum* were also included in the garden. The colchicums were very special. For many years she was the only source of the very rare and expensive *Colchicum autumnale* 'Alboplenum', selling it at 3s.6d. when the Dutch nurserymen

Plate 138. *Gentiana sino-ornata,* like rhododendrons, like a cool root run with an acid soil. Their colour blended very sympathetically with the walls of Balbithan.

Plate 139. *Gentiana acaulis* 'Coelestina', in stages from bud to fading flower.

Plate 140. Rhododendron seedling.

Plate 141. *Rhododendron tephropeplum.*

were usually asking between £10 and £15 per bulb. The pink form of *autumnale* does well in Scotland, in both single and double flowers, along with *giganteum* and *bornmuelleri*. *Colchicum speciosum* 'Album' at 6s. per bulb was an expensive plant in those days.

A particular favourite was *Fritillaria pyrenaica*, its dark purple bells contrasting so strongly with the yellow green of its interior. This flower seems to attract artists; Sir Cedric Morris

Plate 142. Above to below. *Colchicum speciosum* 'Atrorubens'. *Colchicum autumnale* 'Albophenum'. *Colchicum* 'Waterlily'.

Plate 143. *Erythronium dens-canis.* 1978.

Plate 144. *Erythronium. Epimedium.*

Plate 145. Studies of *Meconopsis*. 6.6.96

Plate 146. *Iris foetidissima.*

Plate 147. *Iris unguicalaris* syn. *I. stylosa*. February 2001.

Plate 148. *Iris* 'Katharine Hodgkin'.

brought a form back from the Pyrenees which he distributed widely and both he and Mary enjoyed painting the green changing to gold in the petals. Erythroniums were a great delight. The dog's tooth violet *E. dens-canis*, flowering in March in rose pink and white, gave her immense pleasure. Later these were followed by *revolutum* and *tuolumnense* in white and gold respectively; here the flowers were approaching the form of a dwarf lily. The wild tulip *tarda,* so named because it is difficult to flower, and *batalinii* in soft yellow were accompanied by a

bronze flowering form which Mary enjoyed painting, once again the gold shading to green catching her attention.

Mary's first interest had been in rock garden plants. In my opinion it was their size which attracted. Many of her friends would exchange their recently acquired cultivars and consequently dwarf plants like *Armeria maritima, Androsace microphylla, sarmentosa* and *strigillosa* represented not only a challenge to grow, but a pleasure to pass to other growers. Dwarf campanulas, particularly *pusilla* in

Plate 149. *Iris reticulata.*

white and two shades of blue, were added to the dwarf rock *Dianthus* in the nursery. They would add their splash of brilliant, scented colour in the garden. Epimediums in red, yellow, pink and white would provide graceful colour in April and May, if grown under shrubs and their old leaves cut off just before flowering. This was realised by Phyllis Reiss, a gifted gardener at Tintinhull in Somerset, now a National Trust property. She and Margery Fish worked together with Graham Stuart Thomas to design the border at Montacute House. Epimediums were also a feature of the garden at Balbithan. Mary planted the white *Epimedium pubigenum* in front of the clear yellow of *pinnatum*, making a further colour combination with the deep pink of 'Rose Queen' and the coppery red of x *warleyense*. These, grown under shrubs and with

Plate 150. *Iris winogradowii.*

their old leaves cut off just before they flowered, would provide graceful colour in April and May.

Sometimes Mary would plant in the long raised rockbeds some of the smaller potentillas to flower in May. The saxifrages (Aizoon and Kabschia cultivars) had flowered in March. A small bulb which in the 1960s was relatively unknown was *Rhodohypoxis* from South Africa; its long flowering habit had not yet been recognised. The pink and white of this would blend very comfortably with the dwarf sedums or stonecrops which she seemed to be unable to stop adding to the garden. One of the reasons for this was that the autumn colour of the leaves blended well with the small clumps of the dwarf thymes, whose leaves of bright green, gold and grey started to look a little tired once their flowering was over in July.

Lavenders did not grow easily at Balbithan but, by giving them the very best drainage, she

was able to grow the pale pink dwarf with the 'Munstead' form and her personal favourite of 'Hidcote' with its dark purple flowers in August. *Meconopsis betonicifolia,* the sky blue Himalayan poppy, would seed and naturalize with ease, making visitors from the south stand in amazement if it flowered near the huge five foot (150 centimetre) high flowers of *Meconopsis grandis.* These plants were a great success. Mary knew that much of their success in the garden came from her skill in growing plants and equally that she had carefully placed them in the garden to show their colour in the best possible light of day.

She always gave more importance to the artistic and horticultural placing of her plants. The hellebores were planted in a woodland bed with *Meconopsis* x *sheldonii,* snowdrop bulbs and *Prunus serrula* with its coppery shining bark. Her collection of hellebores was large and of the newer varieties she particularly liked a form

Plate 151. *Iris bakeriana.*

of *Helleborus niger* called 'Potter's Wheel'. This had been found in the Potteries during the war. Miss Davenport Jones and later Elizabeth Strangman of the Washfield Nurseries at Hawkhurst were distributing it. Few of the original clones are still alive but it has led to a strain called 'Potter's Wheel' now being sold grown from its seed. In the case of the *orientalis* group, Helen Ballard and Eric Smith were commencing their breeding. Although I had met Eric Smith, I was not so much influenced by his very superior Constellation hybrids as I was by Helen Ballard whom I visited more frequently because my wife's uncle was a nearby doctor. When she ceased breeding hellebores she sent me some of the plants she did not want to be used for commerce in dwarf black and clear crimson. She said that these were the colours that everyone wanted and that she frequently grew very good cultivars in white

Plate 152. *Iris innominata*. 2000.

Plate 153. *Helleborus orientalis.*

nursery. She never achieved a good colour break as Eric Smith had done with his 'Sirius' which even today is one of the very best of the yellow cultivars.

Mary was never idle. When she was not painting she was gardening and when neither of these occupations could be achieved she was a gifted amateur poet. Her children, grandchildren and great-grandchildren gave her immense pleasure and at the age of one hundred and one she could look back on a lifetime of achievement. Her son John treasured a poem he found after her death and it is, I believe, a fitting tribute to a life which gave so much happiness to many.

The Eident ★ Lass
　　　　★eident = diligent or conscientious

Her love he died at the turn o'the year
(and the long years pass)
Her heart it was broken, she wept for her
　dear
The lonely lass

'Thou didst not wed again', wert thou
　afraid?
(and the long years pass)
'Why, nobody asked me to, sir' she said
(and there's none the marrow of him that's
　dead)
So she thought, alas

She turned to her garden and wrought day
　and night
(and the long years pass)
Her pinks and her primroses all her delight
The eident lass

Her heart that was broken is now made
　whole
(as the long years pass)
And the flowers in her garden cheer many
　a soul
With the birds and the trees and the soft
　green grass
Content, now, she was

Plate 154. *Helleborus atrorubens* was the first of the hellebores to flower, as early as Christmas.

which were equal to the named ones, but there was no demand for them. Mary liked the Lenten rose *(Helleborus orientalis* group) and always considered it a great pleasure to paint. She usually grew several hundred seedlings and flowered them before she sold them from the

Plate 155. *Helleborus niger* Potter's Wheel x *corsicus.*

Plate 156. Seedling hellebore.

Plate 157. *Anemone japonica.* The single white form of anenome called 'Honorine Joubert' (now considered to be a clone of *Anemone* x *hybrida*)was in Mary's opinion the finest of the species.

Plate 158 and 159. *Anemone nemorosa* forms. *Anemone nemorosa,* the wood anenome, grew easily at Balbithan. Mary collected interesting forms which occurred. The pale blue *A. nemorosa* 'Robinsoniana', named after the Victorian gardener, William Robinson, was a particular favourite.

Plate 160. *Clematis tangutica.*

Appendices

Appendix 1

in a trough by the garden door so I can gloat over it.

Yours sincerely, Margery Fish.

From: Mrs. MARGERY FISH.

EAST LAMBROOK MANOR,
SOUTH PETHERTON, SOM.
Tel.: South Petherton 328.

Dear Mrs. McMurtrie,   May 11. 1958.

Thank you very much indeed for the plant of the Hen & Chickens daisy, which I am overjoyed to have, as I love these unusual & interesting plants. You haven't sent me a bill, so I think the best thing I can do is to send you a primrose. I hope you haven't got this hose-in-hose "Darley Beauty". If so please let know and I'll try to find something else. I have had one or two new ones lately — rather new old ones

I am interested in Parkinson's "Paradisus" because I started the enquiry in Gally gaskins. I asked Mrs. Emmerson & she sent me on your reply. I mentioned Gally gaskins in an article & a Capt. Hawkes' wife took me to task & said it was only another name for a Jack in the Green. When I politely asked who was her authority she said her husband! So I am still looking for a gally gaskin or reliable description from some one who's seen one.

Thank you for what you say about my book. I have another in course of publication "An all the year Garden" — mostly overflow from the first. I'll send you a card when it's out.

Thank you again very much. I have put my little

170

FROM : MRS. WALTER G. FISH.

EAST LAMBROOK MANOR,
SOUTH PETHERTON, SOM.

TEL. SOUTH PETHERTON 328.

Dear Mrs McMurtrie   Sept. 7. 1954

I enclose cheque for 2/4, 2/6 &
5 postage on Afterglow. I hope I shall
get Mme Pompadour.

I am having a short holiday in
Scotland with 2 sisters and we are spending
a night in Banchory. I don't know how far
away you are but I'd love to look in and see
you for a brief moment if convenient. It would
be on Sept 28 & 29, but I'd telephone first.

I'd like very much to meet you and
see your garden. I am so involved with
double primroses that I welcome any chance
of meeting fellow enthusiast.

Yours sincerely,
Margery Fish.

FROM : MRS. WALTER G. FISH.

EAST LAMBROOK MANOR.
SOUTH PETHERTON. SOM.

TEL. SOUTH PETHERTON 328.

Oct. 31. 1954

Dear Mrs. McMurtrie,

Thank you very much indeed for the plants, which I am delighted to have.

I am sending you the Cyclamen and the dianthus, but no Mans at the moment as I have had a run on it. But I have just bought 2 more stock plants and will send you some cuttings as soon as I have rooted them.

I am awfully sorry but I have only one BA Purity at the moment and that doesn't look too well.

I went to see Miss Lindsay on Monday. She complains that her Cloth of Gold is looking very poorly and my one plant is too. I wonder what is the matter.

You haven't charged me for the plant of Mme Pompadour, which I am delighted to have, - have priced down the other things more than you should, so I have deducted nothing for these oddments and will send the plants of Mans when I can — Yours sincerely
Margery Fish.

172

Appendix 2

ans. 18 Oct.

Leerne, Limavady, Co. Derry
N. Ireland.
6 Oct. 54 –

My dear Mrs McMurtrie. Thank
you so much for your letter
of 28 Sept. & it is too
sad about B. A. Lilac &
may I please have some
in the Spring? Herewith
a small gift of a pinch
of P. Silverwing seed. I
now remember that there was
next to it in my little cool
house a plant of a very
pleasing unnamed Julia ×
(pale pink) that once produced
a semi-double flower so
we may get something
quite interesting –

yes. would you like to have
1 doz Typh. Purple (rather small
but quite good little plants
I think) for 14/. & send me
in return 1 Downshill En-
sign (for which I think
you charge 7/6) & any Bron.
Accords that you can spare
(whatever you think I deserve
for the jackets.)
I hear Mrs Fish called
to see you. We have cor-
responded for a long time
so tell me what she is like
I imagine her about 40 – very
vivacious with red hair.
I think my Canary H. in H.
are healthy. They grow at a
great rate – but as I told you
they were horrid plants when
they came – All good wishes – W.A.E.

Leck
Limavady
N. Ireland,
12 Dec. 1971

Dear Mrs. McMurtrie

We send our
best wishes for Xmas
and for 1972

And thank you
so much for your
interesting letter of
24 Aug and the nice
drawing of your sun-
dial.

I am still in
hospital. I often go
home for the day &
out to tea parties as
I can get in & out of
the car with help. But
my arm is still very
stiff and awkward &
I am so many simple
things I

cannot perform that
I am grateful to be
allowed to stay on
a little longer. I hope
I'll be home in time
to greet the primroses

I loved the
little booklet, the
the account of the
herb-garden.

Limavady is
quite unperturbed
so far. We have had one
explosion — which
blew up the water-board
office. No one was
hurt.

My husband and
the apparent serve
out the parcels & write
the letters and interfere.

Every good wish

Gladys Emmerson

Appendix 3

Autumn 1 9 6 3.

OLD-FASHIONED

DOUBLE   PRIMROSES,
ETC.

Mrs C. L. EMMERSON, LEEKE, LMAVADY
Co. Derry,   N. Ireland.

No surplus at present of varieties marked x.

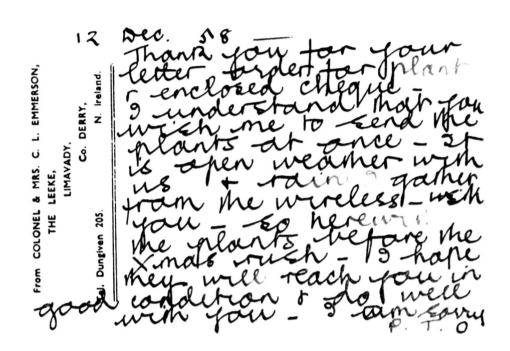

12 Dec. 58 —
Thank you for your letter order for plant
& enclosed cheque
& understand that you
wish me to send the
plants at once — It
is open weather with
us + rain & gather
from the wireless with
you — So herewith
the plants before the
Xmas rush — & hope
they will reach you in
good condition & do well
with you — I am sorry
P. T. O

POST CARD

THE ADDRESS TO BE WRITTEN ON THIS SIDE

that I am practically
sold out of Miss Massey
except for small divisions.
& send 2 for the price
of 1 — they should grow
very quickly —
& am quite sold out
of Burgundy. but I
can get some
in the spring from a friend
by exchange & will let you
know when. & can do anything
French Grey (MO) G. E. Emmerson.

Leura, Limavady, Co Derry
N.I. 7 Feb. 89 –

Dear Mr. Clark –

you noticed here (in
your letter of 4 Dec.)
I have my thing
first – so I enclose
it herewith – You
will notice that
Burgundy is still
off my list but
I am hoping to get
some more of them
(by exchange) They
... it I can get
them, it I'll each
and ... would
would please still start to

have one to not send
the money, until I
know for certain
it I can simply it ...

I am hoping that
I did not make a
mistake over the
single Green throwne –
I always try to not
make mistakes but
my that a single
Green is coming into
flower as B.4 did.
I should have
made a mistake over
you the know the ring
... let the course,
yours very sincerely

(Mrs) Gladys Emmerson

Leeke, Limavady Co. Derry.

1 Mar. 59

Dear Mr. Clark. Thank you very much for your letter of Feb. 3. I shall be pleased to supply 1 plant each of the 3 varieties of Double primrose you mention. Please do not send the money until I send the plants as I do not yet know for certain whether I can include the Burgundy. I am hoping to get some plants from a friend who does not specialize in primroses but has some good Burgundy - but she will not often part with them.

6 Mar. 59

I must apologise for the delay in finishing up your letter but I was hoping for good news of the Burgundy. But I have not managed this. I will send the other 3 plants as soon as I can. I shall hope to include the Burgundy. Please do not send the money till I find out about Burgundy. As it is 7/6 per plant. about the Single Green - let me know. The price is 7/6 per plant.

Yours faithfully - G. E. Emmerson. and regards

what lovely weather!

Leeke, Limavady, Co. Derry N.I.

23 June '60

Dear Mr. Clark — Thank you very much for your order of plants & here they are — You had a credit of 5/6 & the plants come to just £2 — so I have filled in your cheque for £1. 14. 6 —

I have an earlier note to send you another plant of Pompadour but as you do not mention this I do not include it — (I could send one in Aug. if you wish) Our Red Paddy have just been divided &

are very small so I do not include a plant —

We think you have a splendid collection of primroses — I had hoped to send a curiosity but our few plants have been divided & do not look at all right so far. I send the 'Large cream' of Dundalk (a primrose we rarely part with) it have a pale yellow flower the size of a penny. The 'Donabate polyanthus' we only acquired this year from an old garden near Dublin — It is mottled lilac & white, small, but fully double

& we think very pleasing — We hope to find out its history, we just call it the DONABATE polyanthus as that is where it was found. The 'Large cream' is mentioned in Roy Genders' book 'Primroses & Polyanthus'. He had a plant from us & I think he says it comes from Co. Derry — But it was found many years ago in Dundalk. I send several seedlings of the Rose plantain as the ordinary wild plantain so often comes up among them & now you have a margin.

Yours sincerely

G. E. Emmerson.

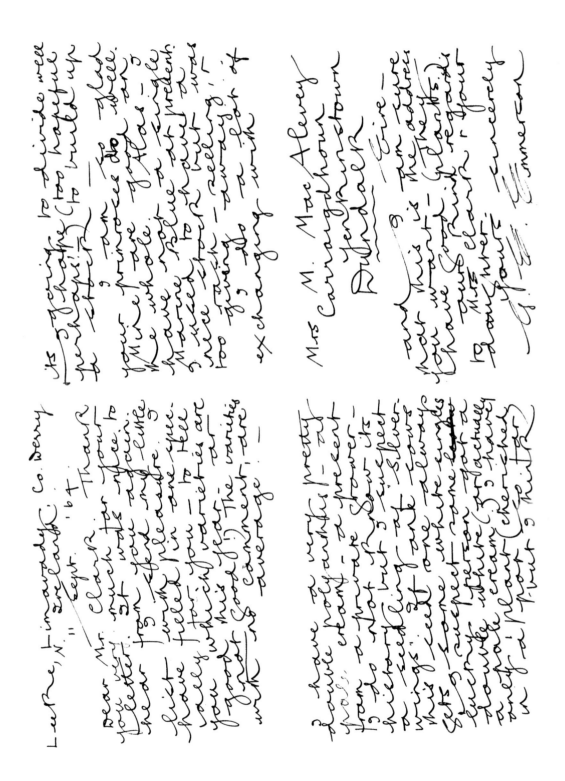

Appendix 4

Mrs. MARY McMURTRIE
SUNHONEY
MURTLEDEN ROAD
MILLTIMBER
ABERDEEN AB1 0HS

29 May '98

Dear Timothy,

What a splendid article for 'The Garden, we were all so thrilled when it arrived, how good of you to have taken so much trouble over it and made it so interesting. So full of information. I don't know how to thank you.

I was so disappointed that I couldn't speak to you on the 'phone when you rang up, I didn't even realise it was you! But I hope to get an improved hearing-aid on Monday — at least they will see if anything can be done.

This has been an exceptionally busy week, with the proofs arriving and a good deal of correcting to be done, and in addition a constant flow of visitors, an exhibition (Tolquhon) to have some paintings delivered (opening tomorrow) and today one of my grand-daughters having a party to celebrate 10 years of marriage and 2 small, lively great-grandchildren here to be looked after this weekend. We have posted back proofs and now await the coloured ones from publishers. It will be such a relief when it is all finished.

I shall be writing again but meantime congratulations, and very many thanks

Mary.

Your negatives enclosed —

Appendix 5

A 25.5.35

22.5.35

Duleek
Co Meath
I.F.S.

Dear Mr McMurtrie

Thank you very much for the
B.A. Purple which arrived
this morning looking fresh
and well.

I enclose Miss Hume's letter
in reference to the double
green primrose — she knows
more than most people about
primroses and told me she
had been 10 years looking
for double green — In about a
month I sd have a plant
to dispose of and wd exchange
with you if you care to do so.

Could you let me have any
Dernclonghi for the double green?
or what wd you suggest.

I have not yet had an
opportunity of tackling the
people about "Harlequin" but
will try and go and see them
soon.

Please return Miss Hume's letter, as I
sd like to keep it for reference.
You will note she is look-
ing for double white Periwinkle? Can
you help? Also I want 1 or 2
plants of the deep purple old
fashioned stock — Hesperis Matronalis
fl plen — I have the double white
and light shade of purple — but
have not the deep purple —

P.T.O.

Do you know of any double
pansies —

Again thanking you
Yrs faithfully
Edith Osborne

I hope the snow did no harm?
we had a shower or two too —

Duleek
Co. Meath
I. F. State

30. 10. 35

Dear Mrs McMurtrie

Thank you for your letter
of a little while ago — I think
we all had a difficult summer
with primroses — just got through
and no more will some Buy them,
If you can spare a Dweloghuy:
even if it looks sad I would
be glad to get it and at treasure
it in a frame glass covered for
the winter — I am in trouly
at least one Rex Theodore "
so may be able to exchange
got something good next
year but at the moment
I should much like a Dweloghuy

Also did you get any double
periwinkles — I think you said
you managed to get double
purple and double blue also?
you get- the white double Bury
if you are selling I would Bury
a plant- of each of the above.
Please remember the customs —
letter postet declared "not"
contain
a letter postet declared "not"
9 days to reach me instead of
possible 2. The packet contained
1 small plant! merecifully beautifully
packed so all was well. If the
contents are declared the parcel comes
on all right. Have you any uncommon
plants suitable for pots?
Hoping you are well

yours sincerely
Edith Osborne
~~~~.

A 11-5-'35   Duleek
Co Meath
. Irish Free State

7-5-'35.
Dear Sir

Thank you for yours, I am sending the plant of double crimson auricula and one or two plants of other auriculas (gratis) which may interest you - The double has been in a glass covered frame, plenty of air, but - I am now getting my plants by degrees out of the glass frame into open frames covered with netting more to keep cats, birds ect out of them - I did not expect any more B.A. blue for I know how difficult it is to get every one of the rarer primroses. Some of the walls of Jericho walk
P.T.O

round and round and round (chiefly by letter) and in the end one generally gets a bit! "The remnants of an "army" one lady remarked, as her primroses having practically all died, she let me have a few plants after months of writing - they too want to keep them till they all die is anytime - Of course keeping them to work up a stock is quite another matter -

Please later on let me have a bit of the B.A. Purpurea when you can spare.
I find one can cut them up rather severely if one puts them in a glass covered frame, pots standing in pans of water and shade from glaring sun - have your double green primroses - I may be able to spare a bit

it got to you!
Please excuse this rather tired
sheet of paper —
If you have a bloom of double
Salmon primrose cd you send
it with the B.A. purple, I am
wondering if the Salmon
is the same as a double Salmon
primrose I once had & knew
where it is still to be had (one
of the walls of Devitto variety)
and I sd much like to see if
the Scotch Salmons is identical.
I am very pleased to send you
the 5/= extra for the two plants
B.A. Blue
Please remember to put "garden
plant only" on outside of parcel
for customs.
                Yrs sincerely
                    Edith Osborne

colr — I have never seen it in
bloom but I got the original
plant from Miss Hunn. (you
may see her letters sometimes
in "Gardening Illustrated") and
she is most reliable, she told
me she was looking for it for
10 years
What cd you offer for a lot of
"Harlequin" exchange. I think I
know where there is some but
don't know if they will part at
any price or exchange.
"Dandelaghi" is a beauty when well
grown bed with gold edge
fades to tortoishell another
grows for it — the bloom I sent
I was jaded when I got it — so it
must have been a beauty when